Critical Guides to French Texts

Critical Guides to French Texts

EDITED BY ROGER LITTLE, WOLFGANG VAN EMDEN,
DAVID WILLIAMS

DURAS

Le Ravissement de Lol V. Stein *and* L'Amant

Renate Günther

Lecturer in French,
University of Sheffield

Grant & Cutler Ltd
1993

ISBN 0 7293 0359 4

I.S.B.N. 84-599-3330-X

DEPÓSITO LEGAL: V. 2.952-1993

Printed in Spain by
Artes Gráficas Soler, S.A., Valencia
for GRANT & CUTLER LTD
55-57 GREAT MARLBOROUGH STREET, LONDON W1V 2AY

Contents

To Catherine

Note

Page references in the text are to the following editions: *Le Ravissement de Lol V. Stein*, Paris: Gallimard (Folio), 1976, and *L'Amant*, Paris: Les Editions de Minuit, 1984.

Introduction

Over the past fifty years, from *Les Impudents* (1943) to her latest book *Yann Andréa Steiner* (1992), Marguerite Duras has produced a large number of novels, 'récits', plays, autobiographical texts and collections of articles. She has also written many film scenarios and since 1969, with her film *Détruire dit-elle*, she has embarked on a second career as a film director.

Despite an apparent thematic continuity, there are several breaks in her work, which can be divided accordingly into a number of distinct periods. The first period spans Duras's early work from her first major novel *La Vie tranquille* (1944) to *Le Square* (1955). In this period Duras introduces a number of themes which reverberate throughout her writing. Her first women characters are already struggling against an intolerable existence, trapped in a prison of social and sexual constraints, waiting for some form of liberation from a state of permanent *ennui*, the monotony of duration which they experience as a kind of death in life. Already the hostile dimensions of time and space, a life of confinement which is always determined in advance and which allows little room for change or expansion, become important thematic elements. However, all of Duras's women characters, both in the early and the later periods, oppose the oppressiveness of their situation by acts of revolt or refusal.

In *La Vie tranquille* Francine's family leads a passive existence, its members destroyed by their own indifference and by time. But the *ennui* which Francine herself endures takes on a particularly repressive form, for as the only daughter she has been condemned by her family to remain 'raisonnable, sage, vierge' (2, p.131). When she incites her brother Nicolas to murder their uncle, she sets in motion a series of changes and begins to question her life and identity. As in *Moderato cantabile* or *L'Amante anglaise*, a dramatic act of violence becomes a catalyst which allows Duras's heroines to escape from their prior state of non-existence. The major part of *La Vie tranquille* is an exploration of Francine's solitary self-discovery during a holiday in a seaside resort. Her questioning of her identity is significant in so far as it announces a central preoccupation in later texts like *Le Ravissement de Lol V. Stein* and *L'Amant*. Francine's interior monologue not only poses the question 'Who am I?', but also reveals a split in the woman's mental self-representation, as she constructs an image of herself as 'elle', 'une autre'. This awareness of the self as divided rather than unified and coherent signals the concern with questioning the traditional Western concept of 'self' which runs through Duras's entire work. The sense of being many 'selves', an infinite number of different forms waiting to come to life, is accompanied by Francine's feeling that she is on the verge of madness, inseparable from Duras's later heroines' experience of the disintegration of 'self'. Like Lol V. Stein, Francine acknowledges that individual identity is perhaps no more than a set of labels and comments that 'mon nom même ne me rassurait pas' (2, p.122). Yet, despite her recognition that the 'self' is not a natural essence but a collection of roles and definitions, Francine ultimately feels that her life has already been determined and that she will never be able to break out of the pattern created by her own past: 'Je suis à jamais prise au piège de cette histoire-là, de ce visage-là, de ce corps-là, de cette tête-là' (2, p.126).

With *Un barrage contre le Pacifique* (1950) Duras wrote her first autobiographical novel, and introduced characters and events which reappear in the play *L'Eden cinéma* (1977) and *L'Amant* (1984). If Francine in the previous novel revolts against an oppressive existence through an individual gesture of violence, the almost mythical figure of the mother in *Un barrage* engages in a struggle against the injustices of the entire colonial system of French Indochina. When she enlists the peasants' help in building a wall against the ocean, she symbolically affirms their collective power against the colonial agents, choosing to act to change her situation instead of accepting her suffering with passive resignation. The novel not only describes the mother's struggle, but also explores the lives of her two children, Suzanne and Joseph. Like Francine, Suzanne feels oppressed by her family, especially her mother, who is described as 'devouring' her. Fantasy becomes a central means of escape from a narrow reality, as Suzanne spends hours in a cinema, seeing her own desire for a passionate love affair projected on to the screen. The films she consumes become a motivating force in her attempts to separate from her mother and to envisage a life of her own choice. The transformative power of art, first introduced in this novel, becomes a crucial element in later works, particularly in *Le Ravissement*, where the heroine's life itself is an ongoing film. However, whilst in the later texts fantasy and reality become blurred, in *Un barrage* they are only juxtaposed. Thus, for instance, the episode describing Joseph's romantic love affair, a typically Durassian encounter, contrasts sharply with the reality of colonial oppression. The anger which motivates both the mother and later Joseph to encourage the Vietnamese people to revolt against, or even to kill, the cadastral agents is a necessary prerequisite for political change in *Un barrage*. As Duras's work develops and more importance is attached to change on an internal, emotional level as an essential part of political transformations, the explicitly revolutionary message of *Un barrage* becomes less relevant.

In the two novels which follow *Un barrage*, *Le Marin de Gibraltar* (1952) and *Les Petits Chevaux de Tarquinia* (1953), Duras explores problems raised by love and sexual relationships. These two novels introduce some fundamental themes developed in later works, for instance, the characters' search for an ideal relationship, the transgression of social rules which this search entails, and the tension between reality and the imagination. The narrator in *Le Marin* breaks out of a conventional relationship and embarks on an adventure with Anna, sailing across the oceans in search of her ideal lover, the 'sailor of Gibraltar', whom we suspect is a fantasy created by Anna. When Anna and the narrator engage in a relationship, the necessity for this fantasy becomes apparent. For the real relationship will only survive as long as it remains precarious, put in jeopardy by the possibility of Anna's discovering her imaginary lover.

A similar scenario is staged in *Les Petits Chevaux de Tarquinia* where Sara, on holiday with her husband Jacques and a group of friends in an isolated resort in Italy, begins to question her fidelity to Jacques and embarks on a brief affair with Jean. The characters in this novel are presented less as individuals than as spokespersons for different ideas on love and marriage. This is the only novel by Duras where the conflict is resolved in favour of permanent monogamous relationships, at least for Sara who decides to accept marriage as her way of life, despite its limitations and the inevitable *ennui*. In *Les Petits Chevaux*, the ideal love which Anna pursues in the previous novel is shown to be illusory, a desire which no relationship can ever satisfy. As Jacques says: 'Aucun amour au monde ne peut tenir lieu de l'amour, il n'y a rien à faire' (5, p.198). There is a certain parallel between Sara and Anne Desbaresdes in *Moderato cantabile*, but whilst the former, after a brief period of questioning her reality decides to conform to it, the latter breaks out of it forever. The refusal which motivates Duras's earlier heroines is only temporary, and novels like *La Vie tranquille* or *Les Petits Chevaux* close with a return to the conventional social order.

Comparing these early novels with some of the texts written in the 1980s one is struck by the sheer difference in quantity. The first novels are long narratives, containing substantial descriptive passages of the setting, of sequences of events, and in *La Vie tranquille*, of the characters' thoughts, feelings and motivations. These realist conventions gradually disappear from Duras's work, and in the 1958 novel *Moderato cantabile* she introduces several new thematic and stylistic features which will remain characteristic of her later writing. In *Moderato* she begins to develop what David Coward has called 'the art of indirect and oblique suggestion' (20, p.59). Instead of a series of events, the novel presents us with a sequence of encounters and elliptical exchanges between the two protagonists, Anne Desbaresdes and Chauvin. Anne's emotional and mental states are never described or analysed, but can only be inferred from certain non-linguistic signs, the way she looks or does not look at her interlocutor, her gestures, her facial expressions. This break with traditional techniques of characterisation continues throughout Duras's later work and represents her first departure from the notion of literary characters as fully rounded individuals.

But it is only with *Le Ravissement de Lol V. Stein* (1964) that Duras undermines all certainties regarding reality and identity. The process of disintegration traced by this novel is embodied in the fragmented abbreviated form of Lol's real name — Lola Valérie Stein. From *Le Ravissement* onwards it is no longer possible to talk about 'characters' in Duras, since the novel finally destroys the very notion of character and with it the concept of 'self' and individual identity. The liberation experienced by Lol V. Stein is no longer a liberation from external oppression, as represented by the family or marriage in previous novels, but freedom from the internal constraints imposed by the demands for one coherent identity. Along with this rejection of 'the self', *Le Ravissement* also inaugurates a decisive break with conventional forms of representation. Whilst in *Moderato cantabile* it is still possible to recognise the setting as part of a particular social reality, e.g. a café in a French seaside town, the places in *Le Ravissement*, S. Tahla, U. Bridge and T. Beach assume a more fantasmatic dimension. They are symbols of Lol's fragmented being, their shortened forms mirroring her own truncated name.

With the publication of *L'Amant* in 1984 Duras continued to question, perhaps more fundamentally than before, the concepts of identity and reality. For if *L'Amant* has been hailed by readers and critics as Duras's autobiography, the book itself as well as Duras's own comments in various interviews, render problematic the very notions of 'autobiography', 'self' and 'the author'. The narrator/ young woman in *L'Amant* is presented to the reader as a series of contradictory images, mirroring the different models held up to her by her family and the society around her. Her 'self' is as fragmented as that of Lol. V. Stein, but in this text Duras's approach to the question of identity acquires a special significance because of its apparently autobiographical status. For reading *L'Amant* means that we can no longer consider a writer as a unified self, 'the author'. The central female figure in the book is not 'Duras', but is herself a 'character', another who is also 'je'.

L'Amant also questions the divisions between autobiography and fiction, reality and the imagination, for in this text reality is seen to be largely reconstructed through language and memory, a series of mental images which mediate the narrator's retrospective visions of herself, her past life and her relationships.

1. Identity and 'Character'

Critics of Duras have proposed two different and apparently contradictory interpretations of the author's conception of female identity and of her women characters' relationship to themselves. Marcelle Marini, for instance, describes Duras's texts as embodying a process of discovering a potential, but as yet undefined subjectivity (*22*, p.18). Other critics, like Madeleine Borgomano, have argued that for many of Duras's female characters the most crucial experience is a loss of identity, a merging of 'self' and 'other' (*19*, pp.139–40). Yet how would it be possible to discard a 'self' which has not yet come into existence? And what would this definition of a specifically female identity be, if not a series of images of what women 'are' or should be?

Le Ravissement de Lol V. Stein describes not so much a woman's discovery or loss of her identity as her resistance to the very concept of 'identity', to the various models she is expected to project as her 'self'. Lol V. Stein suffers from being Lol V. Stein (p.24), a character in a never-changing conventional drama. Yet her real desire is to be a 'nomad' (p.24), moving from place to place, changing roles and identities, but never discovering an ultimate sense of self. And just as she cannot be reduced to one individual 'character', rounded and intelligible, the novel itself defies readers' efforts to compress it into one coherent interpretation. One can nonetheless attempt to elucidate the question of identity in *Le Ravissement* with reference to some of its recurring figures and themes.

The prominent figure of the triangular relationship is a significant element in Lol V. Stein's flight from identity and is central to the 'ravissement' she experiences at the T. Beach ball. Here, as later in *Détruire dit-elle*, Duras creates triangular relationships whilst stripping them of the meanings and feelings conventionally associated with them. Thus, Lol V. Stein does not feel jealous at the ball, indeed she seems to have forgotten 'la vieille algèbre des peines d'amour' (p.19), and Anne-Marie Stretter's appearance, far from prefiguring a relationship of rivalry, is the precondition of Lol's fulfilment.

From within the fairly conventional scenario of *Le Ravissement*, Duras begins to undermine the concept of 'identity' as a set of social definitions and positions in an institutionalised structure of relationships. It is *this* identity that Lol V. Stein wants to lose at the ball, the mask which, in any case, she had never worn with conviction. Freed from her social image by the events of the ball, Lol is not one 'self', but has several 'selves', a being that constantly changes and expands. However, giving up oneself in order to become all others implies a desire for omnipotence, and it is in this sense that the three successive references to God in *Le Ravissement* (pp.47, 49, 51) might be understood. Initially, after the couple's departure, Lol V. Stein is deprived both of her role as Michael Richardson's fiancée and of her sense of being 'one' with the man and the woman. She is reduced to a non-being, 'personne'. But wanting to be 'God' necessitates the reconstruction of the triangle, in which she can again lose her individual persona by incorporating others into herself. Finally, Lol's body stirs in 'the womb of God', signalling her imminent rejection of this non-person, powerless and cast in the role of the victim. But the reborn version of Lol, wandering through S. Tahla in pursuit of the second couple, has already undergone a certain transformation. When Lol disappears in her own fantasy (pp.49–50), Anne-Marie Stretter emerges, and it is from the place of the latter that the new Lol V. Stein constructs the second triangle, where she seems to have the power to transform Jacques Hold and Tatiana. Similarly, at the end of the book, Lol comes to identify with Tatiana until she feels that she is both 'Tatiana Karl et Lol V. Stein' (p.189). Lol's journey through S. Tahla, then, traces the gradual expansion of her identity to include her female doubles. Each process of identification transforms Lol, extending her self-boundaries, until she could be 'vingt femmes aux noms de Lol' (p.105). Geneviève Pellanda, discussing female identity in Duras, arrives at a similar conclusion that 'à travers le corps d'une femme, ce sont en quelque sorte toutes les autres femmes qui parlent' (*23*, p.62).

Yet, in order to maintain the figure of the double, the possibility of seeing herself in and eventually becoming another woman, Lol V. Stein needs the triangular structure, which, in terms of the novel, guarantees the presence of two women. As in a dream or fantasy, Lol's position in the triangle is always split, as she is both the consciousness that sees the other woman and her own image transposed on to her. The only possibility of breaking out of this triangular fantasy would be to reunite the 'subject' and the 'object', the woman and her alienated mirror figure into one 'self'. However, this reunification would also imply a reconciliation of body and mind, of sexuality and selfhood, which are presented as divided entities in the novel. Thus, Lol can only remain the subject of her fantasy and control its various episodes on condition that her body is transformed into 'another', the object of the triangular figure. Being Tatiana Karl and being Lol V. Stein, then, seem to be mutually exclusive within the framework of *Le Ravissement*.

In this novel the concept of the 'individual', firmly located in her or his allotted place in society, is replaced by the idea of a mobile 'self', a hollow form constantly shaped anew by a succession of events and feelings which pass through it. It is this openness which allows Lol V. Stein to be transported, 'ravie', by feelings experienced by others than herself. Yet this almost mystical experience cannot be verbalised, since language itself depends on the differentiation between 'self' and 'other', between the speaker and the addressee. Thus, in Duras's novel, the ultimate word which would abolish all differences, bridging the gap between Lol and the couple, does not and cannot exist. It would have been a word outside language, 'un mot-absence, un mot-trou, creusé en son centre d'un trou, de ce trou où tous les autres mots auraient été enterrés' (p.48). 'Immense, sans fin', the absent word recalls Lol herself. Just as her own name cannot define her, the essence of 'le ravissement' lies in the fact that it can only be felt in a fleeting moment, but not fixed in language. The aural imagery associated with the mysterious word — 'résonner', 'un gong vide' (p.48) — suggests that it is closer to music than to language. At the ball it is music and dance that underscore Lol's experience, and the end of the night, the moment of her separation from the couple, is accompanied by the death of the music (p.21).

Le Ravissement highlights the discrepancies between language and identity. Is Lol V. Stein really Lol V. Stein or rather 'une femme qui pourrait être Lol' (p.151)? Only Lol herself, 'la soi-disant Lol V. Stein' (p.112), understands that names are in themselves empty words which others invest with their meanings. By questioning any 'natural' correspondence that may be assumed between names and persons in the novel, Duras implicitly challenges the idea that language simply refers to a given identity, and suggests that instead language can be used to construct certain definitions of 'identity'.

This is particularly relevant to the question of female identity. Diane Griffen-Crowder, like many other feminist writers, argues that 'woman' is a cultural construct, a set of signs and codes which does not correspond to the fact of being biologically female. There is a discrepancy between the category 'woman' and 'real women' (*36*, p.161). In Duras's novel, the very openness and plurality of Lol V. Stein's being, 'coulée dans une identité de nature indécise qui pourrait se nommer de noms indéfiniment différents' (p.41), imply that female identity can offer many different ways of being beyond the one homogeneous model of 'femininity' offered by our culture. But entering into this 'enchantement', both experienced and created by Lol V. Stein, means that readers will also have to renounce or suspend their belief in their own identities and confront the uncertainties posed by the text.

In *Le Ravissement*, and in *Savannah Bay*, reality is transformed into art — a play, a film, 'l'opéra de T. Beach' — and the characters themselves become artists, actors, narrators or writers, as in *Détruire dit-elle*. Lol V. Stein both creates and enacts roles for herself and others in her 'cinéma', as her past and present reality, the ballroom, her house at U. Bridge and the Hôtel des Bois become a 'stage' or 'screen'. This suggests a conception of being that is always changing, as each new event or relationship brings about a rewriting of the original drama, a change of cast, a different role. Lol V. Stein who rejects all the conventional female identities offered by society — as wife, mother, fiancée or 'mistress' — loses her place in that society, enabling her to participate in her own self-invention. The novel undermines the notion of 'identity' and of 'character' as a collection of personal traits and social definitions. Lol V. Stein can never be 'known', summed up either as an individual self or in relation to the society around her. As Jacques Hold realises, knowing Lol means knowing nothing about her (p.81).

Just as Lol re-creates and transforms herself in her fantasmatic cinema, our imagination as readers becomes transported on to an empty screen, drawn into the blanks in the text, the 'mot-trou' where we can begin to invent our own versions not only of Lol V. Stein herself, but also of those aspects of ourselves that could be Lol.

L'Amant has been considered as a work apart from the rest of Duras's literary production, partly because it has been read as her autobiography. Yet it is not altogether clear whether to classify this text as autobiography, fiction or a mixture of both, and according to what criteria we could slot it into one or the other genre. Marcelle Marini, commenting on these uncertainties, writes that in some press reviews the book has been described as 'à la fois oeuvre de fiction et autobiographie' (*31*, p.7). Perhaps the reluctance which some critics have felt in defining *L'Amant* unequivocally as an autobiography, stems from the fact that in this text Duras questions some of the very distinctions between autobiography and fiction.

Philippe Lejeune, in *Le Pacte autobiographique*, argues that in order for a literary text to be classified as autobiography, the author, the narrator and the central character must be the same person (*39*, p.15). This definition, however, immediately raises a number of questions: How is this triple identity expressed in the text itself? And if we are reading a narrative in the first person, how do we know that the narrative 'I' is the author? Following Emile Benveniste's theory of subjectivity in language, Lejeune suggests that the grammatical first person 'I' is not a concept referring to a particular named individual, but simply designates the person who

is saying 'I' at a given moment. 'I', then, is a position in language
and not a definable reality outside it. However, Lejeune argues that
Benveniste only analysed the first person in spoken, not written
language. If 'je c'est celui qui parle', how would it be possible to
identify a written 'je', the narrator in an autobiographical text?
Lejeune's answer is that 'je' in an autobiography always refers to
the *name* of the author, and hence a work is an autobiography if its
author, narrator and principal character have the same name (*39*,
p.24). This onomastic identity can be established even if, as in the
case of *L'Amant*, neither the narrator nor the central character is
named in the work itself. Such a text, Lejeune claims, is still to be
seen as an autobiography if the narrator behaves as if he or she were
the author. This is true in *L'Amant* where the narrator refers to
herself as the author of Duras's works, including *L'Amant* itself
(pp.14, 25). Furthermore, Lejeune proposes the concept of an
autobiographical contract, 'le pacte autobiographique', between
author and reader, whereby the author has explicitly declared that
he or she is the narrator and main character of the work in question.
Duras's own statements in this respect are somewhat ambiguous, for
whilst she claims in numerous press and television interviews that
the young woman in *L'Amant* is herself, in an interview with
Libération she described the book as a novel (*30*, p.29). This
ambiguity counters readers' and critics' desire to see *L'Amant* as
Duras's 'life story'. The narrator and central character in the book
are not so much 'real individuals' who may or may not be identified
as Duras, as figures in a particular cultural and symbolic pattern,
representing general problems surrounding women's identity. For
this reason, the anonymity of both narrator and character will be
retained in the subsequent discussion of *L'Amant*.

The concept of identity in *L'Amant* is closely related to the
prominence in this book of images, photographs and mirrors
through which the narrator both re-creates and 'destroys' various
versions of herself. This is apparent from the first pages, where she
describes herself witnessing the metamorphosis of her own face, the
rapid transformation of the conventional model of youth, beauty and
wholeness to the image of 'le visage détruit'. This external physical

disintegration could be read as a metaphor for the loss of unity and continuity of selfhood with which Duras's entire work is concerned.

Autobiography itself becomes a mirror, and in *L'Amant* writing about oneself is presented as analogous with seeing oneself. In this sense, the double narrator/character is both subject and object of the narrative and of the gaze which the narrator turns upon herself. This division is apparent not only in the narrator's relationship to her former self, 'la jeune fille', but also in the latter's self-images, reconstructed by the narrator. Looking at herself in a mirror and recognising her sexual attractiveness, she no longer sees herself, but 'une autre' (p.20). Both in *L'Amant* and in *Le Ravissement* this split-off, alienated part of a woman's being is her sexuality which is largely defined in a passive sense, as being seen and desired by men, 'à la disposition de tous les regards'. Seeing herself as if she were someone else, the young woman in *L'Amant* recalls Lol V. Stein's 'voyeurism', as she looks at her double Tatiana through the window. It is as if in Duras a woman's subjectivity, her ability to perceive and act, were incompatible with her sexual being, which becomes exteriorised as a body to be seen. But whilst in *Le Ravissement* this dichotomy is personified in the couple Lol/Tatiana, in *L'Amant* the subject and the object of the woman's gaze into the mirror are anonymous. Moreover, the impersonal passive construction 'comme une autre serait vue' (p.20) raises the question as to *who* is seeing this unidentified 'other woman' in the mirror. Is it the young woman herself who says 'je me vois' or is it rather the eye of 'on' through which she perceives herself? The mirror, then, separates consciousness from the body, as 'je' adopts simultaneously the masculine position of 'tous les regards' and the feminine, alienated place of 'une autre'. Throughout *L'Amant* the narrator's consciousness of identity as a mask or image counters our expectations that this text will disclose the author's 'real self' and thereby satisfy our own desire for a stable identity. The central question in *L'Amant* is not so much a search for an authentic self as the contradictions encountered by the young woman in her attempts to create herself within an already determined set of options. The ambiguity inherent in this process is implicit in the narrator's own relationship to her former self, the young girl crossing the Mekong river, and in the various degrees of proximity and distance between them.

One is struck first of all by the fact that *L'Amant* is written almost entirely in the present and perfect tenses. Although we know that the narrator is writing about herself in retrospect, with a temporal distance of several decades separating the time of narration from the time of the events related, the choice of the present tense gives the impression that the two dimensions coincide, creating a sense of proximity between narrator and character, as past and present become fused into one voice. It seems as if the narrator wishes to abolish all temporal and spatial differences and enter into her own history, experiencing it as if for the first time. She looks at herself as if she were an actress on stage or an image projected on to a cinema screen. Like Lol V. Stein she transforms her story into a film, a sequence of changing self-representations. Rather than 'telling her story', the narrator creates the image, the photograph that was never taken, but which she invents and offers to readers of the book: 'Sur le bac, regardez-moi, je les [les cheveux] ai encore' (p.24). The figure of the young woman, then, is not a reflection of who she *was*, but a set of representations of who she might have been, a partly fictional creation based on both memory and invention. 'Identity' in *L'Amant*, as in Duras's other works, is a flow of constantly shifting images. Yet these images cannot be separated from the social context in which they are 'invented', any more than the narrator can describe herself outside the language of which she is a part. Her self-perception as 'une autre', implicit also in the use of the third person 'elle' or 'la petite blanche', is an expression of her difficulty in situating herself as female in a language and a society that define women as the sexual 'other' in relation to the male 'self'.

'Identity' in *L'Amant* corresponds to a number of points of view, voices and subject positions, all of which can be 'I' but none of which ultimately defines the author's, narrator's or character's 'self'. 'I' can be both the narrator and the young girl, subject and object of the gaze into the mirror, 'l'image absolue' and its creator, the woman's body and the consciousness that sees and describes it. Amongst all these fragmented images, one sentence echoes throughout the book, crystallising the young woman's fundamental desire: 'Je veux écrire'. Writing, then, becomes the one aim which unifies the fragmented self-representations in *L'Amant*.

2. Masculinity/Femininity: Breaking Gender Boundaries

One of the central themes in Duras focuses on an encounter between a male and a female protagonist and on their subsequent attempts, often initiated by the woman, to transcend the boundaries and polarities built into the traditional heterosexual model, and to experience a relationship where each would recognise the other as a complete human individual, complex and diverse. Although this journey towards change is fraught with difficulties, Duras does begin to chart the possibilities of a transition from the culturally dominant gender framework towards her vision of different ways of relating between men and women.

Sharon Willis has drawn attention to the 'conjunction of domination and desire' in Duras's representations of male/female sexual relationships in *Moderato cantabile* and *L'Homme assis dans le couloir (27, p.7). This connection between sexuality and power also becomes a focal element in *Le Ravissement de Lol V. Stein* in the relationship between Jacques Hold, Lol V. Stein and Tatiana Karl. On one level it would appear that Lol projects her desire for self-annihilation on to another woman, Tatiana, and enlists Jacques Hold as the agent of this destruction. However, like Chauvin in *Moderato cantabile*, Hold seems only too willing to accept his part in Lol's scenario.

To understand Lol's involvement and position in the triangle and her role as the initiator of the relationship between Jacques and Tatiana, it is necessary to return to the early part of the novel, the scene at the ball. Lol's experience of loss, her replacement by Anne-Marie Stretter, is the starting-point of a cycle of obsessive repetition. In the second triangle, Lol V. Stein reconstructs her own exclusion from the couple, looking up at the hotel room window where she sees nothing except her own non-existence (p.63). If, in the original triangle, Lol was the 'victim' of Richardson's desertion, in the repeated version of the story she becomes the instigator of the 'ravissement', as she comes to occupy an imaginary position of power in relation to Hold and Tatiana.

However, with regard to the question of gender identities, Lol V. Stein's experience at the T. Beach ball is perhaps fundamentally significant. Whilst, in a conventional sense, Lol is in the position of the victim, in terms of the novel it seems that she experiences her own abandonment rather as a kind of liberation from the constraints of her social role. As Tatiana's comments early in the novel imply, Lol never possessed the persona, the 'presence' which would allow her to be part of a group, whether at school or in society as a whole. Being rejected by her fiancé in favour of another woman, then, displaces her from her position within the romantic love scenario. At the same time this rejection also implies the loss of her gender identity, her feminine status which is dependent on her involvement with Michael Richardson. 'Le ravissement', then, is the counterpoint to conventional relationships, an experience of losing or being freed from the socially defined 'self'. This becomes evident, of course, when Lol herself abbreviates her name Lola Valérie Stein with its feminine resonances to Lol V. Stein, a configuration of letters which has an androgynous or even frankly masculine quality. But Lol's abandonment of her feminine identity also means that subsequently she remains alienated from her own body and her sexuality which she projects on to other women — first Anne-Marie Stretter and later Tatiana Karl.

If Lol V. Stein is the 'absent' woman, neither male nor female, Tatiana is described almost exclusively in terms of her body, contrasting Lol's indeterminate being with a very conventional stereotype of femininity. However, whilst recreating this representation of women, the novel simultaneously undermines it by drawing attention to the way in which it is constructed through language. In a significant passage in the text, describing Jacques Hold's reaction to a phrase said by Lol V. Stein about Tatiana, 'nue sous ses cheveux noirs' (p.115), Duras implicitly questions the relationship between language and reality. What is at stake here is the discrepancy between reality, the simple fact of Tatiana Karl's presence in the room, and language which mobilises a whole network of symbolic connotations surrounding women's bodies and sexuality, transforming an individual woman, Tatiana, into 'woman', a myth assembled from the words spoken by Lol V. Stein. The words 'cheveux noirs' in particular acquire a symbolic significance, since throughout the novel Tatiana's long black hair comes to signify her femininity. Language metamorphoses Tatiana into an entirely fantasmatic figure in Jacques Hold's mind, but his growing awareness that the words 'nue sous ses cheveux noirs' and the vision of Tatiana which they create are entirely meaningless, serves as a form of catharsis. For the text implies that Hold was previously afraid of Tatiana, or rather of his own fantasies about her. Confronting this fantasy and its absurdity together with Lol V. Stein means that he can free himself from it (p.116).

Despite this questioning of the stereotypical identity imposed on Tatiana, neither Lol nor Tatiana herself can disentangle themselves from the real and symbolic structures in which they are enmeshed. Tatiana's wish to regain her lost integrity through love, her vision of 'l'étendard blanc des amants dans leur premier voyage' (p.81) remains a dream, opposed to the destructive reality of her relationship with Jacques Hold. Lol V. Stein, as the spectator in the field, seems at least partly aware of Tatiana's disintegration, as she watches her behind the hotel room window. Her observation that, although they are the same age, Tatiana's body is already damaged, obscures Lol's memories of the ball, as past and present converge in images of death and decay (p.67). Whilst Tatiana remains imprisoned in traditional images of 'woman', Lol V. Stein, by refusing to become Jacques Hold's 'mistress', seems deprived of her sexuality altogether. Within the framework set up by the novel, Lol, in order to recover this part of herself, would have to become 'Tatiana', and indeed, as the story draws to its 'conclusion without a conclusion', Jacques Hold gradually transforms her into Tatiana: 'Lol, près de moi, se rapproche, se rapproche de Tatiana' (p.167). Lol's self-designation as both Lol V. Stein and Tatiana Karl during the love scene with Jacques Hold might signify a reintegration of her sexuality, symbolised by Tatiana, into her previously fragmented being. However, the fact that after the night spent with Hold she urges him to return to Tatiana, and that she herself reverts to her place as the 'third person' in the triangle, indicates that the text does not close with a return to the conventional pattern of relationships, where Lol would gain access to her own femininity by replacing another woman. Instead, she maintains the triangle in which she is neither masculine nor feminine, but genderless.

Roger Fowler in *Linguistics and the Novel* argues that 'texts are structurally like sentences, as well as being constructed out of sentences' (*35*, p.5). This means that narrative categories, such as 'plot' or 'character' could be analysed in terms of the syntax of individual sentences of which the text as a whole is composed. Following this sentence/text analogy, one could suggest that Lol V. Stein's position within the triangular relationship is also reflected in the novel's syntactical structure. If the relationship between Jacques and Tatiana is delimited by the dualistic gender model, the gender ambiguity surrounding Lol V. Stein means that it is often not clear whether she is 'subject' or 'object', 'agent' or 'recipient' of the actions described. This uncertainty is already reflected in the title *Le Ravissement de Lol V. Stein*, which is open to a number of interpretations. The word 'ravissement' itself has at least two related meanings within the context of the novel. It refers, in one sense, to Lol's reactions to the couple's departure at the close of the ball, an event which she experiences as a sort of abduction of herself. This version is substantiated later in the text when Lol says: 'Oui. Je n'étais plus à ma place. Ils m'ont emmenée. Je me suis retrouvée sans eux' (p.138). At the same time, Lol's 'ravissement' is also her sense of ecstasy when she realises that her abandonment by Michael Richardson leaves her free to fulfil her real desire in relation to him and Anne-Marie Stretter — the desire to be the spectator and instigator of their love, rather than a participant in the couple she previously formed with her fiancé. Thus she explains that she no longer loved him when she saw the other woman entering the ballroom (p.137). A conventional scenario, then, where a woman is abandoned by a man, causes an unexpected transformation in the woman herself. In the later development of the story when Lol fabricates the second triangle she becomes the subject of 'le ravisse-ment', as her presence modifies the existence of Jacques Hold and Tatiana Karl and questions their respective identities.

If the syntactical construction of the novel appears to confirm Lol V. Stein's ambiguous position within the triangle, the pronouns used to refer to the narrator emphasise his ambivalence in relation to both Lol and Tatiana. The split image Lol/Tatiana that he creates could be seen as an extension of his own emotional divisions, where the generic masculine 'il' is in conflict with his individual identity, the 'je' that tells the story. Whilst Tatiana Karl, adopting a feminine position in her relationship with Hold, reaffirms his masculinity, designated as 'il', Lol V. Stein's uncertainty regarding her own self seems to offer Hold the possibility of stepping outside the limits of his gender identity. The initial distance between 'il' and 'je' first becomes apparent when the narrator imagines Lol's view of 'l'homme dans la rue', synonymous with all the men of S. Tahla, as the use of the plural indicates (p.55). It is not until the first encoun-ter between Jacques Hold and Lol V. Stein that the narrator's identity is revealed: he is Jacques Hold, 'l'homme dans la rue', confirmed as both 'il' and 'je' through his contact with Lol (p.74). This initial meeting with Lol opens up the narrator's own story, as the distanced narrative 'je' merges with the 'je' of the narrator as participant, as a character in the story. Yet his identity remains precarious throughout the novel. Believing that he has been mistaken and that Lol is, in fact, looking for someone other than himself, the 'je' becomes doubtful and he reverts back to the third person pronoun to denote himself (p.109). From this point onwards, the shift from 'je' to 'il' only occurs in connection with the narrator's accounts of his relationship with Tatiana. In the narration of his encounters and exchanges with Lol V. Stein, however, the 'je' is retained throughout.

In what ways, then, does the narrator's divided identity concern the two women? It appears that 'il' refers mainly to Hold's sexuality, to his masculine position in relation to Tatiana, who, as we have seen, is also described in exclusively sexual terms, albeit as the passive feminine woman. In this sense, 'Jacques Hold' and

'Tatiana, nue sous ses cheveux noirs' are no more than sets of labels, words denoting male and female gender roles. It is only with Lol that Jacques is able to question the authenticity of this identity. The relationship between his name and his being is not a 'natural' correspondence, but a definition from which Lol V. Stein liberates him, just as she later confronts him with his own construction of Tatiana. Thus, when she says his name, the latter no longer seems to define or categorise him (pp.112–13). This questioning of the power of language to define individuals, to imprison them in fundamentally meaningless and arbitrary proper names, nouns and pronouns, is important in Duras's work as a whole. But what seems to be doubtful in the naming scene in *Le Ravissement* is not only the narrator's individual self, but more specifically his gendered self, for the name that Lol pronounces without naming him is the masculine proper name, Jacques Hold.

Whilst the novel suggests that language is instrumental in creating gender positions, in terms of the story itself these positions remain largely unchallenged. Although Lol V. Stein places herself at the periphery of the triangle, she is bound by the rules and codes which shape the relationships within it, as are the other two partners. Caught in the dilemma where she cannot refer to herself as 'je' except as the imaginary subject who controls the triangle from the outside, where she is not 'il' and does not want to be 'elle', she ultimately remains nameless, a cypher, as the letters L.V.S. to which she becomes reduced in later texts by Duras (e.g. *Femme du Gange*) would suggest.

In *L'Amant* a sequence of brief fragmented scenes shows the narrator alternately in relation to her family, her lover and the largely anonymous society at Sadec and Cholen. Each of these relationships in turn contributes to defining both the material choices open to her and her representations of herself, her different roles as daughter, sister and lover. Since none of the characters in *L'Amant*, except Hélène Lagonelle, are referred to by their proper names, their identities are almost exclusively circumscribed by their positions in society and personal relationships. We know little about the lover, for example, apart from his social status as a Chinese millionaire. In this sense, *L'Amant* is closer to Duras's texts of the 1970s and 1980s than to the 1950 novel *Un barrage contre le Pacifique*, since, despite their thematic similarities, Duras uses more conventional techniques of characterisation in the early novel.

Moving from social to individual relationships, Duras creates patterns of repetition and displacement, where the violence and the divisions between people in colonial Indochina as a whole are mirrored in the relationships between the members of the narrator's family, and, to some degree, in her encounters with 'the lover'. Social, familial and sexual relationships are closely intertwined rather than separate areas of experience in *L'Amant*.

In the eyes of the white colonialists at Sadec, the young woman's family represents an unsettling exception to their rules. Although they are white and of French origin, thus belonging to the dominant group, the mother's status as a widow and single parent separates her from the other married white women in the colony. Seen as 'different', she and her family are exposed to exploitation at the hands of the colonial administration as well as to the social ostracism from the French community at the outpost. The abusive gossip about the family is directed primarily against the mother who, by her very position, threatens the traditional family model (pp.108–09). But the disintegrating impact of society on the narrator's family lies not only in the sense of isolation and self-hatred which it has instilled into its members (p.69), but can also be seen more specifically in the internal structure of the family itself, where divisions between 'weak' and 'strong', powerful and power-less individuals reflect the pattern of relationships created by the world outside. The rule of the elder brother within the family, the physical and psychological violence with which he negates and finally destroys the younger brother, become a prototype of power and domination in general. Thus, the narrator explicitly associates the brother's tyranny with her memories of the second world war and the Japanese occupation, where military aggression against defenceless people mirrors on a large scale the relationship between the two brothers (p.78). When the narrator says that the brother wants to occupy 'le territoire adorable du corps de l'enfant, du corps des moins forts', she creates a complex image containing elements of herself, who is 'l'enfant' in the text, of her younger brother and of the lover both of whom are despised by the older brother for their 'weakness'.

At this point it becomes apparent how Duras undermines traditional gender distinctions and replaces them with more intricate and ambiguous representations of 'masculinity' and 'femininity'. Gender in *L'Amant* corresponds less to biological sex than to different ways of being and relating to others. For only one male figure, the elder brother, adopts an exclusively 'masculine' stance. His violence towards all those around him derives from a view of human relationships based on a strict separation between 'self' and 'other', between the subject and objects who become mere extensions of himself. At the same time this obsession with boundaries insists that a clearly defined hierarchy should be maintained, dividing people into 'superior' and 'inferior', 'strong' and 'weak', men and women, while colonialists and the Chinese and Vietnamese people in the colony. Thus, the elder brother not only demolishes the younger, more vulnerable brother, but he also tries to sell his sister as a prostitute (p.94) and to rape his mother's servant and companion Dô (p.28). This pattern of domination continues with his exploitation of the Chinese lover whose very existence is denied during their family dinners at Cholen.

This image of the elder brother stands in marked contrast with the narrator's memories of her relationship with her 'little brother'. The repeated use of the adjective 'petit' to describe both brother and sister points to the similarities between them and creates a relationship where friendship and identification prevail over difference. Throughout their childhood they share each other's experience, be it their adventures together or their common suffering as victims of the elder brother's rule. Their affinity is directly related to their shared opposition to the latter, their common status as 'objects' in relation to him. Both brother and sister, then, could be seen to occupy 'feminine' positions within the gendered hierarchy of the family.

The mother's relationship with her eldest son, on the other hand, is rather more ambiguous, as both a deep sense of guilt (p.97) and a desire for a vicarious share of his power contribute to her obsessive nurturing of him. Her sons' physical prowess is her greatest source of pride, and whereas the narrator loves 'the little brother' precisely because of his vulnerability and lack of power, the mother shares her eldest son's contempt for 'the weak' (pp.71–72). However, there are instances in *L'Amant* where even the narrator herself, despite her hatred of her elder brother, cannot resist the power he wields over the family in the presence of her lover. She joins with the others as they, taking the brother as a 'model' (p.65), exclude the Chinese man from their midst, ignoring him most of the time and remembering his existence only when they need him to pay for their meals. The rules dictated by the elder brother are so pervasive that they completely eclipse and replace the young woman's own feelings towards the lover and her perceptions of him. Like the mother, she comes to accept the brother's hatred of 'weak' men, even though the lover's soft vulnerable body is what attracts her to him. The elder brother's pernicious influence lies not only in his physical domination, but more importantly, in his ability to rule the minds of those around him. In this respect, the parallel which the narrator draws between this individual tyranny and the fascist dictatorship during the war, is clearly appropriate.

When the narrator first meets the Chinese man on the Mekong river, the form that their relationship will take is already in some ways determined in advance, by their respective social situations. By setting their encounters against the backdrop of colonial society and the young woman's family, the narrator questions the assumption that sexual relationships somehow develop between socially neutral individuals. From the outset, the young woman's financial position is inextricably bound up with her sexuality (p.51). The relationship which subsequently develops is in a sense a re-enactment of the relationships that prevail within the young woman's family, as her feelings about her brothers and her mother as well as their attitudes towards her become displaced and transformed into her own ambivalent feelings about herself and her lover. This process of association builds up a complex picture of the central male/female relationship in the text.

In one respect, the young woman and the lover re-create a traditional model of male and female sexuality, where desire is represented as 'masculine' and desirability as 'feminine', reaffirming the dominant active/passive framework. Early on in *L'Amant* the narrator's comments about her own desire confirm this view that female sexuality consists only in the need to be what men want women to be, to become desirable by merging with a generalised image of femininity (p.20). Female desire is represented as negative, as the desire to be desired. When the young woman follows the lover, for the first time, to his apartment at Cholen, she thinks about her desire as an absence rather than a presence of feelings. Sex, then, becomes a kind of obligatory ritual signifying a woman's entry into the social order. However, male/female roles are not as fixed as it might appear at first sight. For soon after her initial reactions, the young woman admits that it was she who found the lover attractive when they met on the boat, and in the ensuing scenes describing their love-making, it is frequently the woman who takes the initiative and expresses her desire for the man. Yet this admission of female desire immediately becomes tinged with guilt, as the narrator describes herself as 'perverted' (p.48). Her expression of her own sexuality allied with the constraints of her economic position do, indeed, transgress the dominant model of the 'respectable' woman. Yet this social division between women in *L'Amant* is revealed as artificial and arbitrary, as all the white women in the colony suppress themselves in order to meet the demands of the men around them, whether their husbands, lovers or the anonymous 'on'. Thus, the married white women spend their lives making themselves attractive for their husbands and are sometimes driven to suicide when the latter discard them in favour of the family's maid (pp.27–28). In this sense, their loss of self is just as total as that of the young woman who asks her lover not to love her as an individual but to treat her as he would 'any woman'. This wish also involves a desire for punishment which, in turn, is presented as contributing to her sexual pleasure (pp.54–55).

On one level, this representation of female sexuality could be seen as a reinforcement of the view that masochism is an inherent part of femininity, and that women themselves consent to or actually demand, as is the case with the woman in *L'Amant*, physical and verbal abuse from men. However, by setting the young woman's experience in a wider social context, Duras implies that this 'consent' is not voluntary, based on individual choice, but rather the result of a complete absence of choice. This is true both in material terms, since the family's poverty leaves her no option other than to become a prostitute, and in emotional terms, as the influence exercised by her mother and her brother on her view of herself also filters through to her way of relating to the lover. The same tension between dominance and submission which inhabits the family becomes part of her first sexual experience. Her ambivalent feelings towards her mother, for example, are frequently invoked during her meetings with the lover, to the extent where at times the lover seems to adopt the mother's role vis-à-vis the child. Whilst, on the one hand, the mother takes pride in her daughter's attractiveness (pp.33, 113), she also hates and punishes her for having sexual relationships. To the young woman herself, then, her body becomes a site of contradictory representations and feelings, attracting both love and hatred, approval and punishment. This ambivalence surrounding her sexuality as such is then repeated in her encounters with her lover. At the same time, the young woman's relationship with her brothers is also transposed on to the image she creates of the lover. This is particularly apparent in the scene where she suddenly thinks and speaks of her brothers in the lover's presence (p.122). Just as the relationship with the lover evokes memories of both 'the hunter' and 'the assassin', the image of the lover himself and his position in relation to the young woman become fragmented and ambiguous. He incorporates both the elder brother's dominance and power and the 'little brother's' vulnerability and suffering. Thus, in the descriptions of the relationship between the narrator and the Chinese man, the traditional gender model assigning opposing positions to both partners, alternates with scenes where the similarities between them are emphasised, creating a feeling of connectedness rather than separation. This process of identification takes place partly through the mediation of a third person, the 'little brother', who shares some of the lover's attributes and experiences, especially in relation to the elder brother. During one of their dinners in the Chinese restaurant, the young woman directly identifies the lover's fear with that of her younger brother (p.66). This creates a triangle of resemblances between the woman and the two men. As with the brother, the narrator shares similar childhood experiences as well as her native country with the lover (p.120).

Whilst on one level the text represents relationships in which the divisions between men and women, the rich and the poor, white colonialists and the Vietnamese and Chinese people, reflect the social realities which frame the narrator's experience, it also creates patterns of interdependence and resemblances between the various characters and relationships it describes.

3. Relationships between Women

The pair Lol V. Stein / Tatiana Karl represents perhaps the most ambiguous and elusive of all the female relationships explored in Duras's texts. On one level, the two women seek in each other the possibility of rediscovering their common memory and experience, symbolised by their shared adolescence at the *collège* and the events at the T. Beach ball, which become an important focus in their later relationship. In this context one brief episode, repeated in the novel (pp.11, 85), is given special significance. On Thursdays, at the *collège*, both Lol and Tatiana refuse to join the ranks formed by the other pupils. Instead they escape to the empty playground and dance together (p.85). This passion for freedom and the women's refusal to be 'put in their place' is resuscitated and mirrored in their later conversations, when Tatiana implores Lol to be her witness and to confirm the reality of their past experience.

The early period of Lol's life becomes associated with her madness, the 'crise' which, according to Tatiana, has always been part of Lol (p.13). It is through Tatiana's observations about Lol, related by the narrator, that we learn of her strange 'absences', her inability or unwillingness to project the persona that others expect her to have. But when Lol, after her later reunion with Tatiana, begins to feign 'sanity' to those around her, Tatiana perceives this ostensible normality as evidence of Lol's continuing illness. For pretending to be 'normal' is symptomatic of her acquiescence to a state of non-being, the disintegration of herself which coincided with her 'recovery' after the ball. Through Tatiana the novel questions and reverses accepted meanings relating to women's madness and sanity. If Lol V. Stein's sanity signifies her submission to and acceptance of her repressed existence, her madness, on the other hand, represents a form of revolt, albeit solitary, against the static passive life that has been imposed on her. Whereas Jean

Bedford, and to some extent, Jacques Hold, feel menaced by Lol's 'folie', Tatiana recognises it as a form of salvation. Since both Lol and Tatiana experience their present lives as a stagnant, numbing form of 'normality', it is not only the survival of Lol's passionate 'madness' which is at stake, but also the survival of the two women themselves.

Their relationship, then, involves partly a reconstruction of their common past, their school-days, their experience at the 'Casino Municipal', in an attempt to find together an escape route from the impasse of their adult existence. Their first reunion ten years after the ball reverberates with resonances of a remote past (p.73). But Tatiana has changed, and it is only Lol who recognises the tiny crack in her voice, this almost imperceptible note of pain expressing the 'crack' in her being. Her laughter and the mischievous spirit of childhood have been crushed by the weight of the present, turning around in endless circles (p.74). Lol V. Stein's understanding of the other woman's emotional state mirrors Tatiana's knowledge of the underlying meaning of her friend's madness, her former passion struggling against the annihilating forces of her social existence — 'son mari, ses enfants, sa maison' (p.76). However, this immediate understanding between the two women is constantly disrupted by the third figure in the triangle, Jacques Hold, who becomes the mediator of the relationship between them. Whilst it appears that Lol has singled out Jacques Hold from the men of S. Tahla partly because he will lead her back to Tatiana (p.115), in their subsequent relationship it is mainly through him that Lol sees and communicates with the other woman. The distancing and distorting effect this has on their understanding of each other becomes poignantly apparent in the only episode in the novel where the women talk to each other alone, during their second meeting at Lol V. Stein's house. The narrator introduces this scene by commenting on Tatiana's need to share her feelings with Lol, the heart which she is unable or unwilling to convey to him (p.89). Momentarily the arrangement of positions in the triangle changes, as Jacques Hold's place remains empty, leaving the women to talk and listen to each other without his presence. Yet his

appearance behind the bay windows and his exchange of glances
with Lol then re-establish the previous triangular pattern and
Jacques Hold's central position within it. Albeit from outside, he
participates in and ultimately directs the women's conversation.
This, incidentally, contrasts with Lol's role as 'the outsider'. For
when she watches Tatiana and Jacques through the hotel room
window she never sees or hears anything directly and needs to rely
on what he chooses to show or tell her. Her perceptions of Tatiana,
and by extension of herself, depend on Hold's representations of
Tatiana, as he 'shows' her to Lol behind the window at the Hôtel
des Bois (p.122). However, in the scene referred to above, Lol
herself adopts this mediating attitude towards Tatiana, opening the
bay window to allow Jacques Hold to overhear their conversation.
Aware of being seen and heard by him, Lol's behaviour as well as
her thoughts and speech then become geared to his presence.
Tatiana, on the other hand, unaware of Jacques outside, continues to
question her friend about the meaning of their experiences as
women and to talk about experiences of her own. Yet, since they
now speak from different positions, their dialogue becomes more
and more disjointed, producing a gap between the meaning of their
respective utterances. For Lol, whilst addressing Tatiana, actually
speaks to and through Jacques Hold (p.93). This discrepancy
between Tatiana's questions and Lol's answers punctuates the
subsequent dialogue and becomes so absurd that Tatiana begins to
interpret it as Lol's pretence, her lies. And indeed, Lol's entire
relationship with the other woman is based on lies, since telling her
the truth about her strange reappearance after their ten-year separation would destroy the triangle that Lol is at pains to fabricate.

Yet the reasons why Lol chooses Tatiana to represent 'the
other woman' in the relationship remain elusive and can perhaps
only be elucidated by returning to the scene of the ball. During the
ball, Tatiana not only comforts and supports Lol, remaining at her
side throughout the night (p.20), but also empathises with and
vicariously experiences Lol's ecstasy, as both of them watch
Michael Richardson and Anne-Marie Stretter on the dance floor. In
the later relationship between the two women, Tatiana's memory,

like Lol's, constantly returns to the ball scene (p.100). But if the ball belongs to Tatiana as well as to Lol, the original triangle might well be seen as a square, since the feelings which circulate during the night at T. Beach affect two 'couples': Michael Richardson and Anne-Marie Stretter and Tatiana and Lol watching them from behind the plants near the bar. Tatiana is Lol's 'double', reflecting her own experience. But even though both women are the same age, Tatiana seems an older 'version' of Lol. If the latter has repressed her desire to live and has always remained on the brink of a potential existence, Tatiana has already arrived at the end of her journey. In this respect she resembles Anne-Marie Stretter at the ball: 'Rien ne pouvait plus arriver à cette femme, pensa Tatiana, plus rien, rien. Que sa fin, pensait-elle' (p.16). But Lol's renewed presence in her life and the persistence of her 'folie' mitigate Tatiana's sense of defeat, as she remembers her old desire to embark on a journey, her own abandoned development. Lol's own journey back to the past, to the T. Beach ball, becomes emblematic for Tatiana's wish to recover her lost potential, to re-experience the happiness of that night. But her possible reunion with Lol is disrupted by a series of separations which mark the women's relationship throughout the book, and which seem to follow a certain pattern tracing the different stages of their lives. Just as temporal and spatial representations in the novel reveal a division between social frameworks, on the one hand, and Lol's emotional experience, on the other hand, the feelings of closeness or distance between Lol and Tatiana also seem to depend on the extent to which Lol either conforms to or resists the expectations of her social environment.

The novel opens with a brief description of the two women's friendship at school, alternating with the narrator's comments on Lol's engagement to Michael Richardson. This period in her life evokes a conventional, almost stereotypical situation, which seems to be in conflict with Lol's 'absent' personality, her constant obliviousness of the roles she is expected to play. The experience at the ball disrupts the predictable path of Lol's existence. Given that the night at T. Beach is shared by Tatiana, Lol's childhood friend, it might be suggested that the ball was also partly a re-creation of their earlier need to live outside all rules and structures, embodied by the couple's freedom to express, albeit for one night, a passion unlimited by social norms.

However, this interlude of closeness between the two women is followed by a ten-year period of separation, as Lol's marriage and subsequent emotional paralysis sever her both from her earlier experiences and from Tatiana, the only person who had shared them. It appears, therefore, that the intimacy between the women coincides with those periods in their lives when they are least restricted by the demands of social conformity.

Throughout their later relationship, which now involves Jacques Hold, Tatiana's efforts to rebuild their former friendship are constantly thwarted by Lol's resistance, her obliviousness of their relationship at the *collège* and even of the other woman's presence at the ball. The position which Lol has constructed for Tatiana, that of her sexual mirror-image in relation to Hold, distances her forever from her friend, making it impossible for her to admit their former closeness (p.96). Through her lie, 'brutal, incompréhensible, d'une insondable obscurité' (p.96), she refuses both to Tatiana and to herself the very evidence of their past, of a time when everything still seemed possible, and which Tatiana hopes to resurrect through her dialogue with Lol. But Lol's façade of contentment with her present existence, shielding her against Tatiana's probing questions, begins to crumble as the two women reminisce about the ball. It is now Tatiana who counters Lol's resistance to her own memory with an account of her friend's real feelings and reactions during the crucial night: 'Non. Je suis ton seul témoin. Je peux le dire: non. Tu leur souriais. Tu ne souffrais pas' (p.99). By revealing to Lol the truth about herself, Tatiana gradually breaks down the barriers of Lol's pretence. The almost therapeutic role she adopts towards her is reminiscent of the exchanges between Alissa and Elisabeth Alione in *Détruire dit-elle*, where Alissa's 'destruction' of Elisabeth uncovers the latter's repressed feelings and memories. As Tatiana and Lol talk about the ball, their speech and memory become increasingly freed from the censorship of oblivion and silence which they had had to impose on their lives.

Although the possibility of liberation for both women is implicit in the novel, it is only with later texts like *Détruire dit-elle* and their destruction of conventional relationships that Duras's women characters are able to challenge the norms which prevent them from relating closely to other women.

In *L'Amant* the emotional ambivalence experienced by many of Duras's female protagonists towards other women is a focal element of the narrator's relationship with her mother. Despite its title the book is largely concerned with exploring the complexities of this relationship.

A number of American feminist writers have regarded the conflictual aspects of female bonding as stemming from the tension between identification and separation which they consider to be fundamental to mother/daughter relationships. Marianne Hirsch, for instance, writes of the desire for female identification and closeness, on the one hand, and of each woman's need to create herself, independently of her mother, on the other hand (*37*, p.202). Similarly, Jane Flax considers the continuity of mother/daughter relationships to be problematic for women's development since 'the inability to differentiate from the mother threatens women's identity' (*34*, p.23). Although these insights are important for an understanding of mother/daughter relationships in general and pertinent to our study of *L'Amant*, the psychological framework which shapes them tends to minimise the social context within which all human relationships, including those between women, are formed. Femininity is a model for identification which severely limits women's choices, prescribing a restricted set of largely biological and/or sexual roles: 'the mother', 'the daughter', 'the wife', 'the mistress'. Yet femininity is also the only acceptable identity available to women, since any other way of being is viewed as 'masculine' and hence sanctioned. This is, of course, important in view of the status of women writers, and provides one of the sources of conflict between mother and daughter in *L'Amant*.

The ambivalence surrounding the central female relationship in *L'Amant* stems from the two women's feelings about their own and each other's femininity, on the one hand, and their implicit resistance to feminine identification, on the other hand. Whilst this conflicting attitude prepares the ground for complicity between them, it also engages them in a continuous struggle with each other. The very image of 'la mère' in the book reflects the narrator's divided feelings towards her. The mother, 'cette femme d'une certaine photographie' (p.21), is described as a powerful woman at the centre of her family, a woman whose sense of despair does not lead to resignation, but motivates her to struggle against the colonial system, and even to build a dam against the destructive tides of the Ocean. The father, on the other hand, is absent from the photographs around which *L'Amant* is written, and even his death is only fleetingly mentioned. Yet the narrator's evocation of her mother's strength and moral integrity is not accompanied by a conventional idealisation of mothering as a role demanding permanent nurturing and availability for a woman's offspring. The mother is described as being frequently so overwhelmed by her despair that she can no longer look after her three young children. The narrator writes with sympathy about these crises, suggesting that their implications for her own later life were positive (p.22). She speculates that her mother's despair might be related to her doubts regarding her entire life, her questioning of her marriage, her relationship with her husband and her children (p.22). These contradictory feelings, alternating between acceptance of her situation and the resolve to fight, become an integral part of the mother's relationship with the young woman. One might surmise that it is partly the latter's understanding of her mother's suffering which motivates her to leave the colony forever and to seek a different existence as a writer. And, indeed, the mother encourages her to leave, not only the colony, but also her place in society (p.32). In contrast with these aspirations for her daughter's freedom and personal fulfilment, the mother encourages her to become a 'prostitute' in order to support the family.

The conflict between the economic and existential constraints imposed on both women and their spirit of non-conformity is implicit in the young woman's choice of her physical appearance and her mother's positive reactions to it. By creating a gender-ambiguous image for herself, combining high-heeled lamé shoes with a man's hat, the young woman not only displays her difference from the other women in the colony, but also infringes upon the codes prescribing feminine appearance and behaviour (pp.19–20). The mother, who originally bought the hat, approves of her daughter's appearance, this 'choix de l'esprit' (p.20), seeing it as a sign of her imagination and opposition to the prevalent norms (p.33).

The narrator's desire both to identify with her mother, and to dissociate herself from her, hinges on two recurring themes in *L'Amant*: sexuality and writing. In one respect, both the discovery of her own sexuality and her wish to become a writer are seen by the narrator as necessary steps towards her own self-creation, and hence, her independence from her mother. But the impossibility of ever completely severing the ties between mother and daughter and of achieving full independence is implicit in the book's intense engagement with the young woman's feelings towards her mother, and the latter's constant presence in her mind, even and especially during her meetings with the lover.

The relationship between the two women reflects a number of oppositions, the 'split images' which, as Adrienne Rich has pointed out, define women as either 'mothers' or 'daughters', creating a false dichotomy between 'identification' and 'separation' (42, p.253). These contradictions, apparent in the archetypal generic 'la mère', set against 'la petite prostituée', depersonalise both women, reducing their lives to two seemingly incompatible choices: either sexuality or motherhood, for as the narrator comments: 'La mère n'a pas connu la jouissance' (p.50). However, the text itself, whilst dramatising these oppositions, also attempts to resolve them. Writing becomes not so much an act of self-creation *against* the mother as a symbolic re-creation of and reconciliation with her. Rather than writing about her mother from the distance which would follow a final separation, the narrator writes *with* her, sometimes adopting her point of view and speaking with her voice. Whilst confirming the existence of the gap between mother and daughter, *L'Amant* allows for a possible reintegration of these two aspects of female experience. Through the book itself, 'the mother' becomes part of a chain of connections, until she is finally synonymous with Duras's own creative process. This integration of the mother's memory into herself and her writing allows the narrator to 'forget' her and the painful struggle between them, as the memory dissolves into the organic associative flow of 'l'écriture courante' (p.38). Writing *L'Amant*, then, is both an act of remembering, recreating the mother/daughter conflict, and an attempt to forget, and by forgetting to heal the split between them. Despite the struggle and ensuing separation between mother and daughter, the mother is one of the few figures in *L'Amant* whom the narrator tries to understand and whom she loves and admires.

Whilst the mother/daughter relationship is central to *L'Amant*, Duras also weaves memories of other women into the book. The successive images of Marie-Claude Carpenter, Betty Fernandez and 'La Dame' illuminate different aspects of the narrator's involvement with and views of other women. Instead of detailed portrayals, Duras draws impressionistic sketches of these female figures, all the more powerful for capturing their presence in a few gestures, a smile, the timbre of a voice. Rather than observing and then describing other women from the detached vantage point of the spectator, the narrator's memories reflect her own emotional closeness to them. Her persistent gaze at Marie-Claude Carpenter, for instance, is a look of recognition, expressing her desire to know and understand the other woman (p.82). The questions surrounding this woman's identity and the reasons why there is this 'particle of death' in her eyes could perhaps help the narrator understand her own secret sadness that has always been part of her (p.57).

The sense of immediate recognition, of a clear female presence in the narrator's memory, is even more striking in the passage evoking Betty Fernandez (p.82). The brilliant clarity of this memory contrasts with the obscurity surrounding the narrator's memories of certain aspects of her childhood, especially her hatred towards her mother. And whilst 'the mother', almost reduced to a nameless category, is seen as a victim, destroyed by society, Betty Fernandez is described as 'souveraine' (p.83). The narrator's perceptions of her and later of 'la dame de Vinhlong' seem to counteract and compensate for the realities of women's suffering exemplified by her mother's experience. The constant incantation of female names — Marie-Claude Carpenter, Betty Fernandez and later Hélène Lagonelle — is almost like an attempt to rescue women from their anonymity and to give them an identity of which 'la mère' and 'l'enfant' have been deprived. Here the association between naming and being becomes so strong that the mere utterance of a name seems to incarnate the woman to whom it is attached (p.82). If the identity of 'la mère' and 'la petite' derives mainly from their place within the family or within sexual relationships, the narrator's wish to know Marie-Claude Carpenter or Betty Fernandez might imply her own desire for a life that is not exclusively tied to this structure. Yet, their 'sovereignty' and self-contained presence also make these women seem displaced, lacking both origins and destinies. Similarly, the sense of mystery which envelops Marie-Claude Carpenter is reflected in her physical appearance, in those dresses which are never 'quite hers'. Like the narrator herself, both women are strangers, both literally, as foreigners in Paris, and metaphorically, in the sense that, as women, all the female figures in *L'Amant* are from 'elsewhere', from the place that Marcelle Marini has called 'les territoires du féminin' (22). The aura of mystery emanating from some of the women in *L'Amant* reflects the feeling of disconnectedness from oneself and other women which Marini has described in an article on the book: 'L'étrangeté à soi est l'un des leitmotive du texte, liée à l'étrangeté pour soi des autres femmes' (31, p.15).

If exile and exclusion are experienced by all women in *L'Amant* this experience takes on a special significance in the imaginary relationship between the young girl and 'La Dame'. For both women have been expelled from their community for having broken its restrictions on women's sexuality. Both have had sexual relationships outside the parameters set by society, and their subsequent punishment links them in the narrator's mind (p.111). Their courage to live in accordance with their feelings and the isolation they suffer as a consequence confer upon them a special power, as they remain 'seules. Des reines', mirroring the stature of Betty Fernandez, 'souveraine'.

The woman who breaks social taboos and lives as an outsider in her society has been a recurring figure in Duras. From the mid-sixties until the publication of *L'Amant* in 1984 this theme of female transgression and exile has become associated with the figure of Anne-Marie Stretter who first appears in *Le Ravissement de Lol V. Stein* and continues to inhabit Duras's written texts and her films (*Le Vice-Consul* (1965), *India Song* (1973), *La Femme du Gange* (1973), *Son nom de Venise dans Calcutta désert* (1976)), until she reappears as 'La Dame' in *L'Amant*. In an interview on *The South Bank Show*[1], Duras confirmed that 'La Dame' was Anne-Marie Stretter, saying that it was she who 'made me an author' and identifying almost totally with her: 'Autrement dit, c'est moi, peut-être'. A figure of identification and source of inspiration, Anne-Marie Stretter reflects Duras's sensitivity to the beauty and presence of other women, underlining the importance in her work of the female 'gaze', clearly perceptible in the film *India Song*.

In Duras, 'looking' often translates a desire that cannot be conveyed adequately through verbal communication. The different ways in which Duras's characters look at each other also express something about how they relate to each other, about the emotional closeness or distance between them. In *L'Amant* this is implicit in the narrator's relationship with her friend at school, Hélène Lagonelle. Initially, the narrator looks at Hélène directly, from the subject position 'je', expressing her feelings of tenderness and desire for her friend (p.89). Her attraction towards Hélène is allied with her understanding and compassion for the other woman's plight, her inability to 'learn her lesson', to be slotted into the place society has already reserved for her. Yet the narrator also knows that Hélène, unlike herself, will not be able to escape from the prison that is being built around her (p.90). The narrator's love for her

---

[1]Interview with M. Duras, ITV, 17 November 1985.

friend resounds in the tender, powerful incantation of her name, as the consonance between Hélène's second name, the initial L. and the pronoun 'elle' creates a melody and rhythm of female identifications: 'Elle. Hélène L. Hélène Lagonelle. Elle fera finalement ce que sa mère voudra' (p.90). Yet the narrator's position in relation to Hélène gradually shifts, as she imagines herself, her friend and her lover in a triangular sexual relationship. This change of perspective is revealing because it mirrors the central contradiction in *Le Ravissement*. If the narrator in *L'Amant* begins by describing her feelings towards Hélène in the context of their friendship, her thoughts about her move towards a depersonalised vision of the female body, 'innocent', but 'powerful', devouring and to be devoured (p.91). This altered image is accompanied by a division in the narrator's self-perception which corresponds, in some ways, to Lol V. Stein's split consciousness in relation to Tatiana Karl and Jacques Hold. As she imagines herself making love to Hélène (p.91), she now identifies with 'the lover', seeing the other woman in the same way as she herself is seen by him, in the room at Cholen. Although she feels attracted to Hélène, she cannot imagine expressing these feelings, other than by substituting 'the lover' for herself and by giving Hélène to him. The vicarious 'jouissance' she then envisages through watching their love-making (p.92) seems to be the only possible way of overcoming this division, albeit in fantasy and through the mediation of a male figure. Whilst calling on 'the lover' to assume her own position as sexual subject, she also needs her own pleasure to be mirrored in that of another woman. The fantasy reflects a dual desire, to love and to be loved, to be simultaneously 'active' and 'passive'. However, given the polarisation of sexuality into opposing gender categories, this desire can only be fulfilled through the narrator's imaginary splitting of herself into the image of 'the lover' and Hélène, allowing her to be both in the 'male' and the 'female' position at the same time. Both in *L'Amant* and *Le Ravissement* the male/female triangle becomes a fantasy mechanism whereby Duras's female figures attempt to reintegrate both aspects of their sexuality and selfhood. It is only in *Détruire dit-elle* that the fantasy begins to become transformed into a potentially real experience, as Alissa attempts to create a more direct and reciprocal relationship with Elisabeth.

4. Time and Space

1. Time

Representations of time in the work of Marguerite Duras are closely linked with the existential situations of her female characters. The recurring temporal motifs in Duras — the destructiveness of duration, the importance of the moment, the merging of temporal boundaries, repetition and return, transition and metamorphosis — can all be seen as reflections of her heroines' realities as women and as attempts to overcome the temporal restrictions imposed on their experience. For instance, the particularly Durassian form of *ennui* felt by almost all her women characters and their subsequent quest for an intense emotional experience, which would liberate them from a lifetime of monotonous sameness, spring from a reality which encloses them within a limited set of choices, allowing little, if any, room for expression and creativity. Few Durassian heroines remain contented with this conventional organisation of their time, seeking to break out of its boundaries by inventing an apparently different, imaginary temporal universe.

Yvonne Guers-Villate distinguishes three attitudes adopted by Duras's female characters faced with the corrosive power of a never-changing continuous present: early heroines, like Francine in *La Vie tranquille*, or Suzanne in *Un barrage contre le Pacifique* turn towards the future, waiting for salvation through marriage or a passionate love affair. Others, like Riva in *Hiroshima mon amour*, Anne Desbaresdes in *Moderato cantabile* and particularly Lol V. Stein, become obsessively enmeshed in a painful experience from the past, whilst only one heroine, Anna in *Le Marin de Gibraltar* seems able to live in and benefit from her present reality. However, this is only possible since the present itself is experienced as

movement and process, embodied in the search for the fictitious
sailor, and not as static duration (*28*, p.363). The young woman in
L'Amant is aware of the destructiveness of duration, knowing that
the intensity of the present moment can only be preserved through
separation, as a memory.

If Duras's women look towards an aim in the future it is
usually a vision of absolute love, in itself, it might be said, a rather
conventional and socially prescribed objective. This is because
Duras is not so much concerned with inventing alternative 'images
of women' as with showing her female characters on a journey of
emotional change. What is important is the moment of transformation itself, the transition from a repressive or traumatic past to an as
yet undefined future. Rather than representing this future vision,
Duras allows her readers to invent their own images of it.

In *Le Ravissement de Lol V. Stein* the time-scale that corresponds to the heroine's social existence is contrasted with the 'inner
time' of her emotional experience. Whilst the scenes in the novel
depicting Lol V. Stein's day-to-day life are compressed into a few
pages, descriptions of the inner world of her thoughts and feelings
are stretched over comparatively long sections of the book. The
period of her engagement to Michael Richardson, for example, is
mentioned in only a few sentences, and the ten years of her life at U.
Bridge are condensed into merely three pages. As Helga Steinmetz-
Schünemann has pointed out, these apparently 'normal' stages in
Lol's existence, related to her integration into society, also signify a
loss of time, the periods when she does not live (*25*, p.339).

The distinction between 'social' and 'emotional' time is
implicit in Duras's use of tenses. All events in the story which
correspond to the socially defined dimensions of Lol V. Stein's life
— her marriage, the birth of her children, her years at U. Bridge —
are related in the past historic, for instance: 'Jean Bedford la
demanda en mariage sans l'avoir revue' (p.30) or 'Lol quitta S.
Tahla, sa ville natale, pendant dix ans. Elle habita U. Bridge. Elle
eut trois enfants dans les années qui suivirent son mariage' (p.32).

Yet within this chain of expected events, Lol V. Stein's
memory erupts, taking her back to the time before her marriage and

the scene of the ball at T. Beach. The immediacy and intensity of this memory create a different present for Lol, indicated by a switch of tenses from the past historic or imperfect to the present tense (pp.44–47). Similarly, Lol's first appearance in the rye-field is narrated in the present tense, relating time to her emotional preoccupations, the intimacy of her imagination. However, as soon as she returns to her husband, the realms of social time and space, the narrative tense shifts back to the past historic (p.66).

The destructive force of social time appears as a central element of Lol's illness following her abandonment at the ball. Days and weeks pass as she finds herself floating in a vacuum, a gratuitous existence devoid of origins, aims or meaning (pp.23–24). Time, then, is experienced as a life-denying force, eventually transforming the woman herself into a machine, as Lol spends ten years creating an artificial order within an absurd existence. 'Etre Lol V. Stein' in the novel means being condemned to a life of stagnant sameness: 'D'une année à l'autre, dit Lol — elle avait un sourire confus — je ne vois rien de différent autour de moi' (p.76). Adulthood, for both Lol and Tatiana, is an endless circle of unfulfilled time, with no hope of change, no possibility of self-realisation.

Whilst in *Le Ravissement de Lol V. Stein* 'social time' is equated with day, and especially dawn, Lol's 'emotional time', relating to her memory, coincides with the night, to the extent where she herself is seen as synonymous with it: 'Elle est la nuit de T. Beach' (p.104). It is during the night of the ball that Lol comes within reaching distance of her only experience of happiness. Yet with daybreak, when the ball comes to an end, social reality intrudes through the windows of the Casino, taking the couple away from her. The night becomes a female domain, where a woman attempts to escape from the rigid regulations of society and create an imaginary universe. This association between women and the night undermines conventional divisions of time according to gender. If women have been confined to daytime activities, leaving the night as a male preserve, in Duras's novel this reality is transformed in a way that makes the night a positive environment for Lol V. Stein, a time for exploration and discovery. The metaphors of day and night,

contrasting reality with Lol's imagination and memory, also differentiate an alienating present from the heroine's desire to return to
her past, to the T. Beach ball. Thus, during her daily walks, she
remains oblivious to the present, as she enters into her own
fantasised 'cinema', the artificial lights of the ballroom.

Lol V. Stein's imaginary re-creation of the ball scene and her
subsequent engineering of a similar scenario involving Jacques Hold
and Tatiana Karl is also an attempt to reorder her past and thereby
to reclaim some control over her present life: 'Et dans cette enceinte
largement ouverte à son seul regard, elle recommence le passé, elle
l'ordonne, sa véritable demeure, elle la range' (p.46). This process
of restructuring the past in terms of her own feelings represents a
certain liberation from her anonymous social existence, reflected in
the 'glacial' order of her house at U. Bridge. Yet, by indefinitely
repeating the past, Lol V. Stein creates a different kind of prison.
The centrality of repetition in the novel has been interpreted by
some critics as a sign of the heroine's desire to return to her
childhood, to a feeling of completeness symbolised by the triangular
figure at the ball. Geneviève Pellanda, for example, has described
the ball at T. Beach as a metaphor for timeless unity and has
compared Lol V. Stein's scream after the couple's departure with
that of a child faced with the anguish of separation from her mother,
'sa chute dans la temporalité' (*23*, p.261). Lol's incessant repetition
of the ballroom scenario might, then, be seen as her refusal to accept
any temporal order, as well as any distinction between individuals,
counteracting her potential self-creation and instead leading to self-
destruction.

Although Lol's movements and actions are repetitive, this
pattern cannot altogether be equated with stagnation or absence of
process. When Jacques Hold says that he accepts 'la fin sans fin, le
commencement sans fin de Lol V. Stein' (p.184), he comments on
the representation of time and being implicit in the structure of the
novel itself. *Le Ravissement* is endless, questioning the tripartite
division of time into past, present and future. Dominique Noguez in
his article 'La Gloire des mots' has suggested that Duras's particular use of repetition, far from creating static circularity, is an

essential element in her conception of writing as search and process (*33*, p.28). By introducing variations into a reiterated phrase or theme, she infuses difference into sameness, and it is the tension between them that both sustains writing itself and mobilises Duras's women characters. For Lol V. Stein, rescuing the ball from oblivion and rehearsing its memory in the present is a vital move in her escape from the paralysing monotony of her married life. At the same time, re-creating the original scene with different actors, in a different setting and with changed roles allows her to move gradually away not only from the past, but also from the destructiveness of the present.

In *Le Ravissement* Duras creates two contrasting forms of duration, as external duration, the socially imposed time of Lol V. Stein's life at U. Bridge and S. Tahla, is counterbalanced by an internal, emotional duration. If the former is represented as a stretch of eventless time, the latter derives its significance from the intense absolute quality of a momentary experience, encapsulated in the moment just before the couple's departure from the ball. Returning in her mind to this privileged instant, distilling each of its seconds, Lol V. Stein builds a different duration, 'l'éternité du bal dans le cinéma de Lol V. Stein' (p.49), transforming a moment in her life into a work of art (p.46). Helga Steinmetz-Schünemann comments on the importance in *Le Ravissement* of self-realisation as a brief moment rather than a permanent state:

> In hardly any other novel by Duras do we see so clearly that what is important is not a lasting way of life but only the moment of coming to life, through the realisation of the self, the end of passive waiting. (*25*, p.341; my translation)

Lol V. Stein herself is aware of this sense of 'awakening', the moment when the immobility of her daily existence finally breaks, when she says to Jacques Hold: 'Je ne sais quelque chose que sur l'immobilité de la vie. Donc lorsque celle-ci se brise, je le sais' (p.130).

However, this does not imply a movement towards a clearly visible and definable alternative, but represents an inner motion, a slow, barely perceptible change in consciousness. As Lol says: 'Nous allons vers quelque chose. Même s'il ne se passe rien nous avançons vers quelque but' (p.130). Change, therefore, is not necessarily bound up with exterior transformations, but proceeds through a form of emotional metamorphosis. S. Tahla remains the same and the external structures of society seem immutable. Yet, within this order, which Lol herself partly reproduces within her own home, another kind of temporal experience contradicts the social divisions of time and reality. This experience is conveyed in the novel through a reversal of conventional temporal distinctions. If the moment is stretched and dilated, relatively long spans in 'objective' time are compressed and only mentioned in passing. In this way, Lol V. Stein's emotional experience is foregrounded through a restructuring of time appropriate to it, whilst the restrictive moulds of the social time-scale are given only minimal attention.

Like Lol V. Stein, some of the women in *L'Amant* experience their lives as an empty suicidal duration, a road already mapped out for them, leading to loneliness, abandonment and even death. The narrator's mother, permanently constructing her children's future, making plans to fill the void of time ahead, 'hurle dans le désert de sa vie' (p.57), whilst the other white women in the colony spend their lives waiting for their holidays or a love affair which would rescue them from their paralysing existence (p.27).

As in *Le Ravissement*, married life for women, especially for Duras's 'bourgeois' women characters, represents a time of numbing stasis, a kind of death in life. Only two women in *L'Amant*, the narrator and Hélène Lagonelle, seem to have the opportunity to escape from this 'law': Hélène because she refuses to grow up, remaining 'attardée dans l'enfance' (p.28) and the narrator because her 'prostitution' makes any future marriage in the colony impossible, thus allowing her to choose a different life, that of the writer. By following her own desire in becoming involved with the Chinese millionaire, she chooses, perhaps unconsciously, not to arrive at the goal set out for her, but embarks instead on a discontinuous path, breaking with the traditional pattern of women's time. As in other works by Duras, continuity and duration are seen as negative aspects of time, eventually destroying the relationship between the lovers. Separation, then, seems to be the only way of keeping their feelings for each other alive (p.119).

Whilst Duras represents the destructive effects of linear, chronological time, she also transforms this conventional pattern, both thematically and structurally. *L'Amant* begins with a lengthy retrospective description of the sudden 'brutal' transformation of the young woman's face, her unexpected ageing at eighteen. Here, time is seen as a powerful disintegrating force, striking, almost assaulting her (p.10). At the same time, Duras reverses the linear framework of time by opening the book with a scene that took place when she was already old, a scene which challenges conventional associations between female youth and beauty and hence the devaluation attached to ageing for women. For out of all the images of herself she accepts that of her 'destroyed face' as that which belongs most closely to her: 'C'est entre toutes celle qui me plaît de moi-même, celle où je me reconnais, où je m'enchante' (p.9).

Linear metaphors of time conveying a sequence of logically related events are replaced by images of open spaces, 'de vastes endroits' (p.14), empty places from which only disconnected fragments of experience can be retrieved through memory with all its gaps and blanks. In this sense, *L'Amant* itself contradicts those critics who have considered the book as a revelation or confession of 'the truth' about the author's life. Marcelle Marini has criticised the view that *L'Amant* is the source or origin of Duras's other fictional works, stating that all writing is necessarily 'une transposition imaginaire' (*31*, p.8), mediating events and experiences. Mingling fact with fiction, Duras weaves some allusions to her previous novels into *L'Amant* when, for instance, the autobiographical 'je' seems to merge with the fictional character of Suzanne in *Un barrage contre le Pacifique* (p.36). Correcting the fictional chronology of *Un barrage* by stating the 'je' met the man in the black limousine after the mother had abandoned her land, Duras, however, contradicts this ostensible fact in a previous passage in *L'Amant* claiming the exact opposite (p.35). Confounding readers' expectations and demands for the knowledge and certainty of an autobiography, Duras reassembles the past through a sequence of images which cannot be fitted into a linear pattern. These images themselves, either as flashes of memory or as an assortment of old photographs, are already representations of the people and events of the past, filtered through the consciousness of those who create and perceive them.

Yet, whilst Duras seems to reject a conventional chronological ordering of events in *L'Amant*, the narrator's reconstructions of her own relationship with time reveals a kind of interior logic, an almost deterministic sense that she always already carries her own destiny inside herself (p.15). Rather than accepting an external 'destiny' forged by her family and society, the young woman follows her own desires against all prevailing norms, since both her affair with the Chinese man and her wish to become a writer infringe the fundamental rules of the society in which she lives. What she carries within herself, then, is her impulse to live her own life, and to express herself both sexually and artistically. This desire creates its own internal chronology, a causal chain of events, as the narrator retrospectively sees the future as being already contained in the present moment. Similarly, the absolute image, had it existed, would already have been part of a future event, the narrator's first meeting with her lover: 'Déjà, sur le bac, avant son heure, l'image aurait participé de cet instant' (p.50).

For the young woman in *L'Amant*, as for most of Duras's fictional heroines, desire is an essential life force. However, as we pointed out previously, what matters is not so much the realisation of desire as the moment of its incarnation. In *L'Amant* this moment is embodied in the metaphor of the river and of 'la traversée du fleuve'. In contrast with the sudden onslaught of time in the young woman's life, the river seems timeless, eternal. Situated between Sadec and Saigon, between family and sexual relationships, the river grants a brief respite from 'real' time. Desire, then, is associated with timelessness, since it cannot be structured and controlled.

In Duras, it is experienced in situations that seem removed from time and reality, like the night at T. Beach or the smile or glance between the lovers in *Savannah Bay*.

In *L'Amant* the ocean, like the river, symbolises both separation and transformation, and both seem to suspend the flow of time. Like the river-crossing, the young woman's voyage across the sea signifies a decisive break with her past, as she approaches an uncertain future. Between worlds and between the different compartments of linear time, the sea becomes associated with a deeply spiritual experience, where all frontiers in space and time melt into a sense of eternity. This experience is evoked in an extraordinary lyrical passage towards the end of the book, a scene imbued with the recurring elements of Duras's imagination: the merging of time, places and identities steeped in silence, childhood memories awakened by music (p.138).

It is only during this period 'outside time' that the young woman is able to remember and recognise in retrospect the full impact of her love for the Chinese man. The meaning of an experience can only be grasped when that experience has already been lost, when present has become past. The narrator arrives at a similar conclusion after her brother's death: that life is only immortal as long as it is alive, but that immortality is only understood through death: 'Que c'est tandis qu'elle se vit que la vie est immortelle, tandis qu'elle est en vie' (p.128). Time in *L'Amant* is fluid, like the river and the sea. If the past remains elusive, present and future constantly hover on the edge of the past, 'perdu dans l'histoire comme l'eau dans le sable' (p.138), and it is only in the eternal present created by the ocean and the music that the narrator can recognise and partially recover from the loss of her love.

2. Space

In Duras the material world and the inner space of emotional experience and thought processes are closely intertwined and reflect each other. But the physical settings in which she locates her women characters are not merely metaphors for their 'states of mind', but directly influence and shape their perceptions of themselves and the world. 'Interior' and 'exterior' space, therefore, relate to each other in real existential as well as symbolic terms.

From a feminist perspective, it is important to stress a third dimension of space in Duras, inextricably connected with the other two: the social and cultural space, the places typically allocated to women in this society. The overlapping relationship between mental, material and social space in Duras produces a corresponding tension between 'inside' and 'outside', as her female figures experience space either as confinement or as liberation, a liberation symbolised by the vast unlimited spaces to which they feel drawn — the sea, the forest, the empty beaches of Duras's more recent texts and films.

'Le vide' is the space from which her female characters can begin to invent themselves and their world. It is represented not only as an empty physical environment but, more importantly, as the imaginary sphere of dreams, fantasies and visions, often condensed in an empty gaze directed at the open space beyond the suffocating fullness of 'civilisation'. Duras's very use of language is linked to this emptying process, for whilst her earliest works still claim to create a sense of plenitude, filling the empty pages with realistic detail and description, her later texts, especially since *Détruire dit-elle*, are almost devoid of representation. Absences, blanks, gaps and the increasing reticence of her characters create a feeling of emptiness, but also convey a sense of freedom to readers, the freedom to invent, to partake in a creative imaginative process, rather than being enclosed in the static representations of more conventional novels.

A crucial element in Duras's relationship to time and space is that both are associated with transition and change, as her heroines find themselves in a kind of no woman's land, between places and identities. This space, which has been described by Micheline Tison-Braun as 'l'entre-deux-mondes' (*24*, p.32), constitutes the frontier between fantasy and reality, absence and presence, and, like the women themselves, eludes any precise description. Lol V. Stein's ballroom, and the Mekong river in *L'Amant* are part of

Duras's spatial universe, where divisions of time and space become blurred, opening up a timeless empty world.

Finally, Duras's women are typically outsiders in their society. Excluded from male public life, relegated to a marginal space, frequently in the traditional female roles, they seem constantly displaced, and, like Lol V. Stein, never quite 'there'. Since they can only be 'present' in a reality which does not answer their needs, they prefer 'absence' and withdraw into a world of their imagination.

Both the mental and the physical space in which Lol V. Stein lives correspond to her relationship with others and with herself, a relationship marked by emptiness and absence, exclusion, confinement and fantasy.

In the opening sections of the novel she is described as a 'non-person', a woman who seems immersed in a kind of mental void. In Tatiana Karl's reminiscences about Lol at school, it is, significantly, her heart, the metaphorical centre of her being, which seems to be missing (p.13). This sense of hollowness in Lol herself is reflected in the peripheral positions she occupies in relation to people and events around her. Her place is essentially that of the spectator, as she sees the world projected on to a stage or screen. From behind the green plants in the ballroom, the windows of her house, the hedge in her garden and later from her place in the field, Lol V. Stein looks at life through her imagination, a life which becomes external to and removed from her. But it is not only Lol who watches her own absence and exclusion. Tatiana, who initially shared her friend's place behind the plants in the Casino, later becomes the passive spectator, at Lol's dinner party, where Lol dances with Jacques Hold in a scene that recalls the night at T. Beach. In both cases, the 'outsiders' are women, whereas the male characters are at the centre of the event.

However, Lol's absence and exclusion cannot be considered entirely negative, condemning her to a state of total passivity. On the contrary, it is her very outsider status, her own sense of being 'different', which eventually enables her to escape from her restrictive real environment into the 'other' space of her imagination, where she is not only the spectator, but also the 'metteur en scène' of the relationship between Hold and Tatiana (*21*, p.285). She simultaneously watches and produces her own 'cinéma', combining her previous passivity with active creativity.

Lol V. Stein's emotional space is the antithesis of the material space in which she lives, as the strict order in her houses at U. Bridge and S. Tahla clashes violently with her own inner turmoil, her passion and restlessness. But however much Lol herself attempts to stifle her need for freedom and movement, by imposing exaggerated structures on the space around her, the house itself, despite its 'glacial order', remains infused with her passion (p.34). The house in *Le Ravissement* becomes a stage where the conflict between Lol's desire and the demands for conformity to a certain social model is enacted. On the one hand, both the house and the woman herself become imitations of this model. Yet Lol commits one striking error in this apparently flawless construction of herself and her environment: she arranges the paths in her garden in such a way that they do not join up. This error, quickly corrected by Jean Bedford (p.35), reflects the fragmentation of Lol's being, its division into separate, disconnected compartments.

Throughout *Le Ravissement* the image of the house represents both Lol V. Stein's real physical imprisonment and her sense of mental confinement. Locked up in her house at S. Tahla, even her thoughts are kept under control, as none of them is allowed to cross the threshold of the house, synonymous with her mind (p.45). Mental and physical space become equivalent since Lol's social environment incarcerates both her body and her mind. The house, therefore, is not simply a concrete physical image conveying an abstract mental state, as Duras blurs the very distinction between concrete and abstract, material and emotional realities.

Houses and towns in *Le Ravissement* also become alibis of Lol V. Stein's social acceptability, façades behind which she hides her 'madness', her 'passion absolue'. However, the façade cracks more and more, and no matter how convincingly Lol utters the place names which vouch for her 'sanity' — U. Bridge, S. Tahla — the 'other' Lol V. Stein becomes visible both to herself and to Jacques Hold (p.146).

If the house represents Lol's mental and physical enclosure, the place which traps her 'inside' social norms, the street signifies the beginning of her search for freedom. However, the street connects her not so much with the outside world, the society of S. Tahla from which she chooses to remain aloof, as with her own memories and fantasies. The street is the place where she is able to 'give birth' to her hitherto 'sterile' repressed thoughts (p.45).

But walking the streets also reinforces Lol's 'outsider' position vis-à-vis society, as she returns to the forbidden place of her memory, the ball at T. Beach, different, like the young woman in *L'Amant*, from the world around her. In both texts, this difference of the women characters is translated by a spatial image, placing them 'de l'autre côté du fleuve' (*L'Amant*, p.93). Lol is said to be 'de l'autre côte du large fleuve qui la séparait de ceux de S. Tahla, du côté où ils n'étaient pas' (p.42).

Houses and streets, enclosed and open spaces, correspond to two fundamental aspects of Lol's existence in the novel, as she leaves 'l'immobilité du songe' and begins to wander aimlessly and happily through S. Tahla. Movement and change seem to be ends in themselves, as Lol's attraction towards the outside reflects her need for constant mobility. From this point of view, her return to the rye-field after the episode in the hotel room at T. Beach could be seen as her refusal to become confined to interior spaces. Looking up at the window of the Hôtel des Bois, she looks into her own fantasy, her private 'cinema' or 'opera'. The field, then, unlike the house or the hotel room, seems to be her most intimate space.

Yet whilst Lol's preoccupation with the ball scene and her involvement with Jacques and Tatiana allow her to escape from the real limitations of her social existence into her imagination, fantasy itself can become yet another form of confinement. Just as she imagines being able to wall up the memory of the ball, sealing all the windows (pp.47, 49), Lol herself is locked up inside her own obsessions, separated from others. Her flight into fantasy can be seen as a form of liberation only in so far as it gives her a sense of personal freedom and creativity compared with her suffocating domestic life. However, the rigid pattern of the fantasy itself seems to preclude any changes in her real life.

Like Lol herself, hovering on the brink between fantasy and reality, always partly inside and partly outside society, the physical locations in the novel, the towns of S. Tahla and T. Beach, seem half-real and half-mythical. Both places are sometimes described in literal terms, as the dwelling places and holiday resort of the local bourgeoisie (p.40), and sometimes as regions of Lol V. Stein's memory (p.42). In her conversations with Michelle Porte in *Les Lieux de Marguerite Duras*, Duras said about her own (unconscious) creation of the name 'S. Tahla' that its real meaning was 'thalassa', the sea (*12*, p.85). The sea in Duras's work has been interpreted by some critics as a symbol of the desire felt by many of her female characters to return to the mother/daughter relationship, to 'la mer matricielle' (*23*, p.267). Perhaps Lol V. Stein's 'madness' as well as her 'ravissement' spring from the contradiction between this desire, central to her fantasy about the ball, and its impossible realisation. At the same time, this tension is crucial to Lol and other women characters in Duras, for it is the mobilising force in their journey, impelling them to move on constantly, deferring and transferring their desire without ever reaching its 'end'.

Images of the sea and the river are central to *L'Amant*, symbolising separation, transformation and discovery. If, traditionally, men have travelled the oceans, whilst women have stayed behind taking responsibility for the survival of their communities (p.132), in *L'Amant* it is a woman who refuses to stay, who leaves her lover, just as she had previously separated from her family. The narrator's voyage across the ocean signifies both an experience of loss and separation and the recognition that separation is necessary for her own continued search for herself.

However, if the river and the sea embody the narrator's break with her past and her exploration of new horizons, it seems that it is only the experience of change itself, the passage between the two banks of the Mekong, and later, between the continents of Asia and

Europe, that allow her to feel free. For as soon as she arrives at the other side of the river, entering the lover's room at Cholen, the family from which she had hoped to liberate herself returns to her mind as the image of her mother becomes an almost physical presence in the room. The room is inhabited by shadows, fusing her present situation with the past, when she imagines her mother's own childhood, fraught by a painful event to which she merely alludes (p.50). This room, then, like the rooms in *Le Ravissement de Lol V. Stein*, is transformed into a setting for an imaginary triangular relationship. In this scenario, the narrator's mother is alternately witness and participant, identified with her daughter as 'the child' and distanced from her as a figure of authority, enforcing society's laws and threatening to punish or even kill her.

Like Lol V. Stein's ballroom, the room at Cholen is compared to a vessel, 'embarquée dans la ville' (p.52), lost within the ocean of the surrounding world. The relationship between the lovers cannot be closed off from the society of which it is a part and which intrudes through the paneless windows into their private space: 'Aucun matériau dur ne nous sépare des autres gens' (p.53). Lol's 'navire de lumière', the lovers' room in *L'Amant* is 'shipwrecked', vulnerable to the pressures of the social order which will eventually destroy their relationship through its racist prejudices. If the boat on which the young woman crosses the river seems to promise a new life, free from social and familial constraints, the room at the other side of the river, surrounded by the noise of the town as if by the sea (p.55), symbolises the wreck of this vessel of freedom: 'C'est un lieu de détresse, naufragé' (p.56). Threats of death pervade the room at Cholen, linking it with another room, in the mother's house at Sadec, where the young woman is beaten, punished for living her sexuality. At Cholen, in the 'garçonnière', she herself demands physical punishment from her lover. Sadec and Cholen, the woman's place within the family and her sexual relationship, merge into a space of violence, guilt and loneliness. Rooms in *L'Amant* become a metaphor for the complexity of the narrator's relationships, the ambivalence of love and hatred, contradictions which can never be fully understood, like a room whose door is forever closed (pp.34–35).

In *Le Ravissement de Lol V. Stein* the heroine oscillates between the 'inside' and the 'outside', between the social conformity symbolised by the confinement of her houses and the freedom of the streets, the rye-field and the sea at T. Beach. The narrator in *L'Amant*, on the other hand, seems to be a perpetual 'outsider', as she and her family live on the fringes of white society in the colony. Early on in her life, she already describes herself as exiled, displaced, everywhere in the streets, the towns, available to anyone (p.20). The family is compared to a house, a structure whose walls have crumbled under the impact of poverty and oppression imposed by the colonial administration (p.58). For the young woman's mother this state of exile has transformed life itself into an eternal desert, a vast arid space devoid of hope or expectations of a different future. The recurring image of the desert (pp.57, 59), usually related to the mother's empty existence, also describes the narrator's vision of her own life in the colony. However, the desert, like the suffocating rooms at Sadec and Cholen, also becomes the source of her desire for freedom and creativity (p.126).

The image of the river with its connotations of movement and change counterbalances the eternal monotony evoked by the desert. Representing a link between the past and the future, between the narrator's family and her lover, the river's symbolic significance derives from its intermediary position. Bracketed out of social time and space, the Mekong is equated with discovery, with the journey towards a new world. It is in this transitional space that the narrator experiences moments of profound understanding. In the retrospective account of the river crossing, for example, she realises the total implication of this episode in her life, her own awakening which could have been fixed in 'l'image absolue'. Yet as soon as the crossing is over, and the young woman steps across the threshold of her lover's apartment, this process of change becomes arrested and even reversed. Her existence as a woman, her sexuality, her relationship with the man are cast in the same mould that defines her position within the family, and this makes the two banks of the river seem like mirror images of each other (p.93). Finally, it is only by undertaking another voyage, a second crossing of frontiers, that she can leave behind both places of the past and begin a new life as a writer.

5. Style

Metaphors, Key Words and Symbols

Marguerite Duras's writing has been a gradual process of reducing themes, images and syntactic constructions to minimal forms of expression. From *Détruire dit-elle* onwards, all extraneous elements have been removed, as her style preserves only the core of an experience, the essence of a feeling. She replaces the clutter of traditional novelistic representation with a blank screen; and what she calls 'le bavardage romanesque' (*26*, p.141) is replaced with a background of silence, against which minute sensory experiences become magnified and intensified. *Le Ravissement*, compared to later texts, still contains a fairly substantial number of images and complex syntactical forms. These images can be divided into several groups involving a number of discrete elements which create an overall pattern of metaphors. Each of these patterns will be discussed in turn and linked to thematic aspects of the novel.

1. Liquids

Reading *Le Ravissement*, one is struck by the prevalence of images which incorporate water or liquids in various forms. Early on in the novel, Lol V. Stein herself is likened to water, as Tatiana Karl describes her already strange, indefinable being as a young woman at the *collège*: 'Tatiana dit encore que Lol V. Stein était jolie, qu'au collège on se la disputait bien qu'elle vous fuît dans les mains comme l'eau...' (pp.12–13). From the beginning, water is the metaphorical equivalent of Lol's fluid, boundless way of being and her resistance to any of the identities into which society attempts to mould her. The sea mirrors her wish to break through the barriers of the self and merge with the world around her, just as the sea merges with the sky at T. Beach (p.186). The ocean also becomes part of a metaphorical pattern expressing Lol's unfulfilled desire to embark on a voyage with Michael Richardson and Anne-Marie Stretter. The ball is the symbolic vessel which would carry all three towards an unknown place of Lol's dreams, an impossible future togetherness, as they remain in the harbour of the present. She imagines the ball as 'ce navire de lumière sur lequel chaque après-midi Lol s'embarque mais qui reste là, dans ce port impossible...' (p.49).

As with the ocean, Lol V. Stein has a special affinity with rain, in whose formless monotony she discovers 'cet ailleurs, uniforme, fade et sublime' (p.44). The adjectives 'fade et sublime', evoking both the rain and the 'other world' of Lol's imagination anticipate a later passage in the novel where her words are likened by Jacques Hold to 'insipid milk' (p.106). Here Duras has created an intricate web of metaphors where liquids as a central element come to represent both Lol herself and her words. Like the rain, the metaphorical 'milk' of her language is hazy and unfathomable. This sense of obscurity, of a state of mind where all boundaries have dissolved into a 'lait brumeux et insipide', is reiterated later in the novel in connection with Lol's memory: 'Je n'essaie pas de lutter contre la mortelle fadeur de la mémoire de Lol V. Stein. Je dors' (p.182). The repetition of 'fade' or 'insipide' serves not only as a metaphorical device, to describe certain aspects of Lol as perceived by the narrator, but also has the structural function of linking thematic elements in the novel, e.g. Lol's lack of and resistance to a clearly delimited identity, her gradual oblivion of her past, and the novel's questioning of language as a means of defining and ordering the world. The term 'fade' in connection with Lol's memory and her words expresses in concrete, sensual terms the longing for a state of non-differentiation from others and the world which underlies Lol's 'ravissement' at the T. Beach ball.

A look at a second group of metaphors confirms our view that Duras uses certain, what might be called 'fusional elements' as metaphors for Lol V. Stein's desire to break down the barriers between herself and others. These elements can be divided into three groups: mud, mist and magma. Jacques Hold sees in Lol's eyes a mixture of water and mud: 'Ses yeux sont veloutés comme seuls les yeux sombres le sont, or les siens sont d'eau morte et de vase mêlées' (p.83). The reference here to 'l'eau morte' and to the 'douceur ensommeillée' in Lol's eyes points to the deadly side of her life, that of the 'dormeuse debout' (p.33), the silent passive woman whose feelings and desires have been swallowed up by the muddy monotony of her everyday life. In a later episode Lol herself seems to have the power to transform Jacques Hold's heart into mud, to weaken him to the point where he will fall asleep (p.111). When Jacques dances with Lol at her party, he feels as though the transparency of her eyes suddenly turns to steam or mist, as Lol drifts off into a hazy area of her own fantasy, an area which he will never know or understand (p.155). Both mud and steam are created out of a mixture of elements, water and earth or water and air, as each loses its distinct properties. Associated with Lol V. Stein, these mixed elements provide an apt metaphor for her own lack of recognisable characteristics. The most striking image in the novel of this process of merging concerns language and occurs when Jacques Hold dreams of abolishing language itself, melting down all individual words into one incoherent mass: 'Je voudrais faire, dire, dire un long mugissement fait de tous mots fondus et revenus au même magma, intelligible à Lol V. Stein' (p.130). Only the so-called Lol V. Stein herself who eludes language as an instrument of classification would be able to understand, paradoxically, a language which would no longer be one, a 'magma' of words without distinct meanings. Even sounds would lose their individual quality and blur into 'un long mugissement'. This passage echoes Lol's earlier dream of an absolute word, a word which does not exist as such, because it is beyond language, a 'mot-trou' which no one could utter, but which would resound like a 'gong vide' (p.48).

Le Ravissement already announces the destruction of language and the privileged status of music and silence in Duras's art which assume an even greater significance in *Détruire dit-elle*. Lol V. Stein's passive refusal of the identities proposed to her goes hand in hand with her transgression of a logical coherent language. As we have seen, her urge to break away from both language and society, her dream of 'un ailleurs', is sometimes expressed through metaphors relating to water and various liquid elements, suggesting the indistinct world of her imagination.

However, liquids are frequently opposed to the solidity of ice and stone, as the dissolving power of water contrasts with images of glaciation and petrification. These images are particularly striking in the passage describing Lol's domestic life at U. Bridge and later S. Tahla, where both the rigid external order and the constant suppression of her feelings make her entire world seem like a vast expanse of solid ice. Similarly, her oblivion of her past is compared to a slow freezing process, 'la lente, quotidienne glaciation de S. Tahla sous ses pas' (p.61). But images of winter and ice also imply their opposites, as the awakening of Lol's passion is compared to a melting or cracking of the 'glaces de l'hiver' (p.34).

2. Birds, Wind, Flight

A second group of key metaphors in *Le Ravissement* is centred around images of birds, of flying and of gusts of wind or air sweeping through the stifling atmosphere of Lol V. Stein's daily existence. The symbolic meanings surrounding bird metaphors hinge on the themes of freedom, women's transgression of the sexual morals of society, and death. In one of the first scenes in the novel, Anne-Marie Stretter, whose appearance at the ball parodies the stereotypical 'femme fatale', is seen by Lol as embodying 'cette grâce abandonnée, ployante, d'oiseau mort' (p.15). A rather more complex metaphor suggesting the image of a bird appears later in the scene describing Lol's first reunion with Tatiana since the ball. Their shared adolescence and anticipation of the future have disintegrated into a uniform present, and the narrator describes Tatiana's cry as 'le doux cri aux ailes brisées, dont la fêlure n'est perceptible qu'à Lol V. Stein' (p.74). The contradiction between the freedom of the past, when Tatiana's laughter filled the dormitories of the *collège* and the constraints and emptiness of her adult life is movingly expressed in this description of her cry as a bird with broken wings. Similarly, Lol's suppressed desires are likened by the narrator to 'wild birds'. Engaged in a superficial exchange about her houses and parks, she suddenly becomes immobile, and the narrator's speculations as to her thoughts are couched in metaphors about wind and birds in flight (pp.145–46).

3. States of Mind/Body Metaphors

There are many instances in *Le Ravissement* where an event or a state of mind is described either as a physical presence or as a sensation felt by the person experiencing it. Through this transposition from abstract mental categories to concrete physical reality, feelings become palpable, at times even visual and accessible to the reader's senses through Duras's creation of a particular kind of metaphor. One example of this is the use of the word 'couver' in connection with Lol's illness (p.12). Both the verbs 'couver' and 'éclore' are related to gestation and birth, literally to 'hatching', and form part of a set of metaphors translating the transition from formlessness to form, from Lol's 'nothingness' to her multiple identities. The use of 'couver' suggests that her illness is a living being, a part of her which had always existed in embryonic form, but which had been stifled by the affection shown to her by her entourage. This type of imagery gives a physical presence to Lol's inner experience, contrasting with her apparent lack of personality. Whilst she appears to be 'nothing' to those around her, she secretly 'hatches' her own emotions, giving birth to the 'other' version of herself. Early in the novel, the idea that this second Lol V. Stein is about to come to life is condensed in the phrase: 'Puis un jour ce corps infirme remue dans le ventre de Dieu' (p.51).

Stephen Ullmann, in *Style in the French Novel*, has suggested that an author's choice of 'vehicles' to convey certain ideas may allow readers to draw 'specific conclusions' about the author's underlying psychological or philosophical preoccupations (*43*, p.216). The imagery in *Le Ravissement* frequently involves a process of substitution of vehicles relating to the body or physical, sensual experience for mental processes. Duras's choice of images, in this case, seems not only to embody areas of the mind, but also to blur the very distinctions between body and mind, concrete and abstract. This imbrication of the mental and the physical, of 'inside' and 'outside' is apparent, for instance, in the description of Lol V. Stein 'entering the ball': 'La lumière des après-midi de cet été-là Lol ne la voit pas. Elle, elle pénètre dans la lumière artificielle, prestigieuse, du bal de T. Beach' (p.46). The image suggested is of Lol entering into her own vision of the lights at the T: Beach ball, as if phenomena that take place inside the mind were projected outside and changed into a material reality. If, on a thematic level, there is a division between mind and body, symbolised respectively by Lol herself and Tatiana, on a stylistic level this dichotomy seems to disappear through the prominence in the novel of mind-as-body metaphors.

Unlike *Le Ravissement*, *L'Amant* presents us with few images or metaphors. Instead the book resounds with words that, through their constant repetition, create distinct symbolic patterns. These charged words, for instance 'l'amant', 'la Chine', 'le fleuve' or 'l'oiseau', are repeated like an incantation, acquiring different connotations as the text flows on. The sense of connectedness between people and places in *L'Amant* stems directly from Duras's mode of writing. The image of the Mekong river could be seen as a metaphor for a style which she has called 'l'écriture courante'. The power of this current is perceptible in the process of reading itself, because it carries the reader along. The fluid quality of Duras's writing works directly against any attempts to stabilise the characters, feelings or relationships she evokes, as fixed categories are given mobility, change shape and finally mingle with each other. But writing is also closely bound up with the narrator's desire to live, create and express herself. The repeated evocation of the river combines with the image of China to create a complex symbol of desire in *L'Amant*. Just as the river collects and absorbs everything from the surrounding countryside, sweeping away 'tout ce qui vient' (p.30), all the tensions and contradictions, the mixture of tenderness and violence which surrounds the narrator's relationships with both her mother and her lover, become part of and dissolve 'dans le torrent, dans la force du désir' (p.55).

The question of colonialism and racism, although not developed explicitly in the text, appears throughout, often implicit in the repetition of the word 'blanc' in its various contexts. Here 'blanc' has both the referential meaning of 'white skin' and the metaphorical meaning of 'white dominance'. However, the literal and symbolic levels of meaning in *L'Amant*, as elsewhere in Duras, are identical, for in the social and political context of the book, whiteness automatically entails power over the Chinese and Vietnamese people.

A rather enigmatic symbol in Duras and which appears in both *Le Ravissement* and *L'Amant* is the bird, sometimes associated with freedom, with childhood and at other times with death and madness. The bird in *L'Amant* becomes a symbolic link between the death of three members of the narrator's family, representing three different generations. A bird lost in the father's study is the sign that announces his death even before the telegram is received (pp.41–42). Similarly, the narrator's recollection of her grandfather's death conjures up images of birds: 'Les deux étaient morts aux dates et aux heures des oiseaux, des images' (p.42). Later the narrator's reflections about her brother's death and their childhood are suddenly interrupted by a stark and eerie description of birds screeching in the cold wind (p.130). There seems to be no contextual link between this passage and the preceding ones, and it can only be understood symbolically. The phrase 'des oiseaux crient' and the word 'déments' associate the bird images in *L'Amant* with a second theme and character — the mad beggar-woman who crosses the immense tropical forests and finally arrives at the sea: 'Un jour elle est face à la mer. Elle crie, elle rit de son gloussement miraculeux d'oiseau' (pp.107–08). A single word, then, in this case 'l'oiseau', can grow into a complex polysemic symbol, condensing a number of thematic strands. The narrator's childhood relationship with her brother, the violence and absurdity of his death and the life of the beggar-woman, condemned to madness by the colonial society around her, are all reflected in this image.

Paradox

The use of paradox is a common stylistic device throughout Duras's work and appears to varying degrees in the two texts discussed here. Duras, through her creation of particular kinds of metaphors and symbols, questions a way of thinking that is typical of Western culture and that divides the world into dualistic categories, e.g. body/mind, nature/culture, emotion/reason, masculine/feminine. The frequency of paradox or oxymoron in Duras is an indication of her preoccupation with these apparent oppositions and of her attempt to disrupt their logic through the ambiguity of her style.

One distinction which Duras consistently undermines through the use of paradox is that between presence and absence, between concrete visible form and an invisible emotional world. In *L'Amant* there is a rather strange passage about a photograph which has never been taken because no one, except God, could have predicted the importance for the narrator of the event which this photograph would have captured and eternalised (pp.16–17). However, it is precisely from its absence that the missing image derives its absoluteness. Duras might be saying here that the real importance of the river crossing, its 'absolute' quality in terms of the narrator's entire life, can never be expressed or represented. All forms of representation, whether verbal or visual, are ultimately inadequate, and the essence of a feeling, the total significance of an experience lies in itself, and not in what can be said about it.

There are numerous examples of this particular paradox in *Le Ravissement*, involving an apparently contradictory co-existence of absence and presence, as in the following sentence: 'Les yeux rivés à la fenêtre éclairée, une femme entend le vide — se nourrir, dévorer ce spectacle inexistant, invisible, la lumière d'une chambre où d'autres sont' (p.63). These paradoxical images are a stylistic reflection of the novel's questioning of certain concepts and ideas which privilege presence over absence and plenitude over emptiness, as, for instance, the idea of a whole uncontradictory self or of knowledge as an instrument of explanation and mastery of the world. Duras's female characters, on the other hand, undergo a constant process of loss, of their identities, their memories and their security. In *Le Ravissement* the paradoxical conjunction of terms connoting presence or fullness with words referring to absence and emptiness suggests that the stripping away of accepted values and forms of knowledge can be an enriching experience. In the following description of Lol's walks through S. Tahla, the word 'l'oubli', referring to her progressive loss of memory and self, is juxtaposed with 'fastueux', evoking a sense of opulence: 'Elle commence à marcher dans le palais fastueux de l'oubli de S. Tahla' (p.43).

A second group of paradoxes in *Le Ravissement* focuses on the figure of Lol V. Stein herself, her lack of an easily definable personality and hence her mystery to others. Jacques Hold's comment that knowing nothing about Lol means knowing her already (p.81) is taken further in his later observation that he can only be profoundly mistaken about her (p.169). Lol V. Stein confounds all the rules of common-sense logic, since in the novel knowledge is the absence of knowledge, becoming oneself involves losing 'the self', and the power of 'le mot-trou' lies in its non-existence. In this sense, Lol could be seen as an allegorical figure for the breaking down of the conceptual world of Western cultures typical of Duras's work as a whole.

Metonymy

It is generally accepted that the use and understanding of metaphor rely on the perception of similarity in dissimilarity, a relationship of sameness and difference. Metonymy, on the other hand, is based on contiguity, on the perception of proximity or remoteness between phenomena. David Lodge has defined it as 'a figure in which the name of an attribute or adjunct is substituted for that of the thing meant, e.g. sceptre for authority' (*40*, p.76).

The metonymic images in *Le Ravissement* are often close to what Stephen Ullmann has called 'elliptical personification', i.e. a form of metonymy where an action is substituted for its agent or a quality for its bearer (*43*, p.141). This figure tends to personify certain attributes and abstract them from the person to whom they belong or with whom they are associated. In the following sentence in *Le Ravissement*, for instance, Lol looks at Anne-Marie Stretter's gracefulness rather than at the woman herself: 'Lol, frappée d'immobilité, avait regardé s'avancer, comme lui, cette grâce abandonnée, ployante, d'oiseau mort' (p.15).

There are also instances in the novel where metonymic imagery has the function of transferring one aspect of experience to another. The passage describing Lol's reawakening thoughts about the ball (pp.45–46) contains both metaphor and metonymy. On one level, the idea of the ball in Lol's mind is compared to a body, clinging to the woman who nourishes and protects it. But at the same time this metaphorical body is also part of Lol herself, i.e. of her memory, and the substitution of 'the ball' for 'Lol's memory of the ball' is a metonymic one. Considering that it was Lol's own body that was symbolically murdered by Michael Richardson's betrayal at the Casino, this entire passage might be seen as a series of metonymic displacements involving Lol's body and mind, in the sense that her body becomes displaced on to an experience associated with it, i.e. the ballroom scene which, in turn, is transformed into the image of a body.

Another example of this combination of metaphor and metonymy is the description of the Casino Municipal towards the end of the novel (p.176). The image of the giant bird serves not only as an appropriate means of representing the shape of the Casino, but also as an echo of similar images which appear earlier in the text. As we have seen, the image of the bird is associated with all three female figures in the novel and hence its repetition in this context can be seen as a metonymic link, through which the Casino becomes connected with them. And indeed, for all three the Casino is the place where a decisive event, the night of the ball, occurred. This association between people and places can develop to the extent where characters become places as in Jacques Hold's comment regarding Lol V. Stein: 'Elle est la nuit de T. Beach' (p.104).

Despite these examples of the use of metonymy in *Le Ravissement*, the novel remains primarily a metaphorical text. *L'Amant*, on the other hand, has been described by Duras herself as a 'constant metonymy' (*29*, p.93). The image of China in *L'Amant* creates a network of similarities between the people who are part of it. The narrator herself, her lover and Hélène Lagonelle, despite their differences, all belong to China. Thus, the man comes to resemble Hélène through the narrator's association of both of them with China (p.92). People become linked in the narrator's or reader's mind through similar gestures or activities, or through their shared connections with other people and places. The images of Marie-Claude Carpenter and Betty Fernandez mirror each other as the narrator recalls — or imagines — both of them looking at 'les catalpas en fleurs' and 'les rues vides de l'occupation allemande' (pp.81, 85). This association between people is also established through shared characteristics. Although Duras never makes a direct comparison between the narrator, her mother and the beggar-woman, a certain affinity between them is implied in the references to madness in relation to all three women. This link is suggested through the repetition of the word 'folie' and through successive shifts in the narrative focus. The narrator's recollection of her childhood fear of the beggar-woman, 'la folle de Vinhlong' (pp.103–04) is immediately followed by a brief allusion to her fear of her mother's madness (p.104). The subsequent memory describes the narrator's own experience of madness when she felt that her mother was no longer her mother (pp.105–06). Part of the structural and thematic coherence of *L'Amant*, then, lies in this metonymic web formed by the narrator's memory of the people and places of her adolescent experience.

Syntax

Perhaps the most idiosyncratic feature of Duras's writing is her syntax. It is her particular combination of words, the rhythm of her phrases and the gradual disintegration of the syntactic order that give her style its individual quality. In *Les Parleuses* Duras said that for her words were more important than syntax, and that her words, rather than forming the logical links in a syntactical and narrative chain, were meaningful in themselves. The sentence follows the words, organising itself around them (*10*, p.11). An important aspect of Duras's style, which remains constant throughout her work since the sixties, is her preference for nominal syntax. In *Le Ravissement*, for instance, we find many sentences where a verb or an adjective has been transformed into a noun or a noun phrase, as in the sentence 'J'apprends que le naturel du rire de Lol est incomparable lorsqu'elle ment' (p.86) or 'L'approche de Lol n'existe pas' (p.105). In the last sentence the verb 's'approcher' has been changed into the noun 'l'approche' which then becomes an adjunct of Lol — 'l'approche *de* Lol'. Duras tends to substantivise actions or attributes in such a way that they appear to become autonomous entities. This is partly due to the fact that she is less concerned with individual 'characters' than with generalised patterns of human interactions and experiences. The importance of these patterns is foregrounded by deleting 'the subject' and by transforming movements, attributes and feelings into agents rather than mere adjuncts. Thus, the characters in *Le Ravissement* seem determined by events and by their own feelings rather than determining and controlling them. This tendency to assign a privileged place to feelings and sensations, to the visceral level of human life, might be interpreted as a reflection of Duras's questioning of the desire for a controlling rational 'self'.

The particular quality of Duras's writing is perceptible not only in her syntax, but also in her mode of description. Durassian description is typically sparse, capturing the impressions experienced by the observer of a scene rather than the scene itself in all its complexity. In the passage depicting Lol V. Stein's return journey to T. Beach, for example, a few words — the sea, the train, a purple haze — are linked together in a simple yet very powerful image (p.176). The impact of this description stems from its simplicity, and from the fact that the elements which comprise it are never actually represented. Duras does not tell us what the sea or the sky look like. In the same way, there are no explicit descriptions of Lol V. Stein in the novel, either of her physical appearance or of her emotional being. In Duras people and things simply *are*, and their particular qualities may depend on who perceives them and how. Hence each reader can invent his or her own image of the above scene, from the outline which Duras provides.

In *L'Amant*, of several striking descriptive passages, the scene that captures the narrator's river crossing, is particularly worthy of analysis (pp.29–30). To begin with we see only a misty scene infused with one colour: the pink light which radiates from the young woman's hat. There is a gradual progression in the construction of this scene, as we move from visual experience to a more tactile, physical sensation — the river flowing like blood through the narrator's body. Finally, there is a shift to aural perception, as a number of noises are introduced into the description. Duras uses either very ordinary verbs or deletes them altogether. This extreme form of nominal syntax emphasises the quiet static exterior of the scene, contrasting with the emotional undercurrent which sweeps through the work as a whole. The visual quality of this setting, the juxtaposition of light and colour, is reminiscent of images from some of Duras's films, e.g. *Aurélia Steiner*, with its shots of the Seine glistening under a constantly changing light.

The narrative and syntactical framework of *L'Amant* could be described as one vast sentence, a progressive accumulation of words and syntagms which briefly capture the narrator's impressions and then dissolve into other words, new images. Glimpses of understanding, fragments of memory seem to become transferred directly from the narrator's consciousness on to the page. The syntactic rhythm of *L'Amant* is broken and halting, suggesting the difficulty of imposing order and continuity on the narrator's memory. It is as if, when describing a particular image or event, Duras starts from nothingness, from a background of silence and emptiness. From this void one or two isolated words emerge, tracing the contours of the scene about to be described. More words are added until the whole picture begins to take shape, as in the narrator's reflections on departures and voyages: 'Les départs. C'était toujours les mêmes départs. C'était toujours les premiers départs sur les mers' (p.132).

Julia Penelope and Susan Wolfe have proposed a number of stylistic features of what they describe as a feminist aesthetic. These would include 'parallel structures, short simple sentences, frequent repetitions, conjoined phrases and clauses characteristic of cumulative style' (*41*, p.133). This definition would seem appropriate to Duras's style, especially her syntax, and her aesthetic could, therefore, be said to mirror a certain feminist vision. This vision is guided by a need to break out of the rigid hierarchical structures of our society. The different components of Duras's style can all be seen to contribute to this process of opening up more diverse forms of language and experience.

Conclusion

Duras's work can be seen as a gradual process in which such concepts as 'the self' and 'gender identity' are questioned and broken down. At the same time, Duras increasingly eliminates from her writing all traditional elements, like 'character' or 'plot', and abandons any concern for 'realistic' representations of events or of the temporal and spatial settings she creates. The anonymity of both characters and setting in later texts like *La Maladie de la mort* (1982), *L'Homme atlantique* (1982) or *Emily L.* (1987) invites us to read them as allegories rather than as reflections of the experiences of isolated individuals.

Duras is, of course, not the only modern writer who challenges traditional views of 'the self'. As Gabriel Josipovici has shown in *The Lessons of Modernism*, this 'letting-go' of the self is part of an ongoing trend in twentieth-century literature in general, a reaction against a particular concept of the self prevalent in Western societies since the seventeenth century, according to which 'the self is seen as a stronghold, clearly bounded, well defended by powerful walls, buttressed by possessions' (*38*, Preface, p.x).

Marguerite Duras, in her conversations with Xavière Gauthier, alludes to the anguish she felt in writing *Le Ravissement de Lol V. Stein*, a fear which she describes as 'dangereuse un peu' (*10*, p.14). It is possible that this anguish was in some ways connected to the experience of 'letting go' of the self with which the novel is concerned. Yet, how can we survive without this fixed identity to hold on to and without all the patterns of behaviour that maintain it intact? Duras, instead of providing a direct answer to this question, seems to suggest that perhaps it is necessary to go through a period of destruction, a time of confrontation between traditional ideas of 'self' and especially of the gendered 'self', and radically different ways of being and relating. Duras's women characters in particular live in this transitional world, where they are suspended between the necessity of destroying an existence and a self-image which threaten to destroy them, and a future which is, as yet, unknown. The new concept of 'self' which Duras envisages through her writing is never the stable, self-contained 'ego', separated from others. On the contrary, it is a way of being that is open to the outside, receptive to and moving towards others. For Duras this is not only a personal but also a political necessity, a means of overcoming social divisions and hierarchies based on a rigid self/other polarity. In her works, it is almost always women, like Anne-Marie Stretter or Lol V. Stein, who are prepared to take this first step. Perhaps this is because they have so little to lose. Lol V. Stein loses a 'self' which was, in any case, never quite 'there', and Anne-Marie Stretter renounces the approval of the colonial society from which she feels already completely separate. Duras's women characters, because of their marginal position, their non-identity and exclusion from society, set an example both of how to let go of 'the self', its boundaries and possessions, and of how to move towards what Duras has called 'le point zéro' (*32*, p.51), the point where all existing knowledge has been destroyed or forgotten. Her own writing which has been a constant process of elimination, of reducing linguistic, narrative and thematic structures to a minimum, reflects her characters' movement towards 'le vide', from which a different society, different ideas about the self and about human relationships might emerge.

L'Amant: a Note on the Film

In January 1992 a film version of *L'Amant*, directed by Jean-Jacques Annaud, was released in cinemas throughout France. Like Annaud's two previous films, *L'Ours* and *Le Nom de la rose*, *L'Amant* achieved instant commercial success and, in this respect, it seemed to mirror the recognition won by Marguerite Duras's book in 1984.

Given Duras's longstanding career as a film maker it was surprising, however, that she was not involved either in directing this film or in writing the screenplay, which was co-authored by Annaud and Gérard Brach. Partly due to ill health, Duras had agreed to collaborate with Annaud in an advisory capacity only, but soon felt that the screenplay did not do justice to her original text. A bitter quarrel ensued, until Duras finally distanced herself from the film and wrote her own cinematographic version, published in June 1991 as *L'Amant de la Chine du Nord*.

Within the context of our study of *L'Amant*, the main question raised by the film concerns the extent to which Annaud has succeeded in conveying both key narrative and thematic elements and the distinctive aura that emanates from Duras's book.

From a structural point of view it is interesting to note that various details and scenes included in the film do not appear in the 1984 version of *L'Amant*. The 'paso doble' scene at the 'pension Lyautey', the brothers' names Paulo and Pierre and the extensive description of the young girl's first journey from Sadec to Saigon in the black limousine, for instance, are all taken from *L'Amant de la Chine du Nord*. It seems, then, that Duras was disinherited twice of her material, including parts of her own 1991 'counterversion'.

Some of *L'Amant's* thematic preoccupations have been convincingly transferred to the screen. The marginal status of the lovers, condemned by a racist colonial society, the ambivalence of tenderness and violence underlying the narrator's relationship with her mother and her lover, the mother's despair, are portrayed perhaps even more vividly than in the book, since the realism of Annaud's images adds a concrete tangible quality to Duras's often rather abstract style. The scenes depicting the famous family dinner at Cholen or showing the mother's pain at her eldest son's departure, are amongst several moving examples of the film's emotional expressiveness.

On the other hand, the centrality in the book of the narrator's journey of self-discovery has been largely overlooked. Apart from Jeanne Moreau's intermittent readings of first-person narrative passages from the text, there is little indication in the film of the complex and fragmentary nature of the young girl's emerging identity. Similarly other female characters in *L'Amant*, significant in the narrator's search for selfhood, are relegated to the margins of the film. Anne-Marie Stretter is glimpsed in two brief snapshots and hence the sense of complicity between the two women in the book is almost entirely lost. Hélène Lagonelle features in the early scenes of the film, but substantial sections of the 1984 text referring to this figure have not been included. Thus Annaud did not choose to have Moreau read the incantation of Hélène's name, one of the most poetic passages in *L'Amant*, nor is there any allusion to the imaginary triangle that links Hélène, the narrator and the Chinese lover. Again this is an important omission, since the figure of the triangle in Duras represents the blurring of identities and ambiguity of subject positions which is a crucial thematic aspect of both *L'Amant* and much of her previous work.

The relevance of Annaud's film to the book lies mainly in its evocation of the atmosphere that envelops the young girl's relationship with her lover. Filmed on location in Vietnam, *L'Amant* captures the tranquillity of the Mekong, the dusty desolation of the plains, the heat, noise and claustrophobia of Cholen and Sadec, all of which are central motifs in the text. But whilst Annaud's meticulous attention to external detail may satisfy some viewers' desire for realism, the film lacks the suggestive elusive quality of Duras's writing and of her own cinema.

Much of the publicity surrounding the release of *L'Amant*, particularly in Britain, created the impression that this was a film based on a semi-pornographic confession novel. Whilst initially expressing some of the sensuality, passion and emotional turmoil in Duras's book, the lengthy and explicit sex scenes in the film distract from other crucial aspects of the text and do little to counterbalance the commercial sensationalism with which the film was marketed. A vast financial enterprise, *L'Amant* may have attracted international audiences, but overall it does not reflect the complexity and subtleties of the book. Perhaps only Duras herself can successfully film Duras.

Bibliography

Unless otherwise stated, the place of publication of items in French is Paris.

A. WORKS BY M. DURAS REFERRED TO IN THE TEXT

1. *Les Impudents*, Plon, 1943, reprinted Gallimard, Coll. Folio, 1992.
2. *La Vie tranquille*, Gallimard, Coll. Blanche, 1944, reprinted Coll. Folio, 1982.
3. *Un barrage contre le Pacifique*, Gallimard, Coll. Blanche, 1950, reprinted Coll. Folio, 1978.
4. *Le Marin de Gibraltar*, Gallimard, Coll. Blanche, 1952, reprinted Coll. Folio, 1977.
5. *Les Petits Chevaux de Tarquinia*, Gallimard, Coll. Blanche, 1953, reprinted Coll. Folio, 1973.
6. *Le Square*, Gallimard, Coll. Blanche, 1955, reprinted Coll. Folio, 1990.
7. *Moderato cantabile*, Minuit, 1958.
8. *Le Ravissement de Lol V. Stein*, Gallimard, Coll. Blanche, 1964, reprinted Coll. Folio, 1976.
9. *Détruire dit-elle*, Minuit, 1969.
10. *Les Parleuses (entretiens avec Xavière Gauthier)*, Minuit, 1974.
11. *L'Eden Cinéma*, Mercure de France, 1977, reprinted Gallimard, Coll. Folio, 1989.
12. *Les Lieux de Marguerite Duras (avec Michelle Porte)*, Minuit, 1977.
13. *L'Homme atlantique*, Minuit, 1982.
14. *La Maladie de la mort*, Minuit, 1982.
15. *L'Amant*, Minuit, 1984.
16. *Emily L.*, Minuit, 1987.
17. *La Pluie d'été*, P.O.L., 1990.

B. SUGGESTIONS FOR FURTHER READING

Books and Theses on Duras

17a. Barbéris, Dominique, *Marguerite Duras: Moderato cantabile/L'Amant*, Coll. Balises, Nathan, 1992.

18. Borgomano, Madeleine, *Duras: une lecture des fantasmes*, Cistre, 1985.

19. ——, *Une écriture: Marguerite Duras*, thèse pour le doctorat ès lettres, Université de Provence, Centre d'Aix, 1979.

20. Coward, David, *Duras: Moderato cantabile*, London, Grant & Cutler, 1981.

21. Didier, Béatrice, *L'Ecriture-femme*, PUF, 1981.

22. Marini, Marcelle, *Territoires du féminin: avec Marguerite Duras*, Minuit, 1977.

23. Pellanda, Geneviève, *Figures de la femme dans l'oeuvre de Duras de 1968 à 1978*, thèse de doctorat, Université de Provence, 1980/81.

24. Tison-Braun, Micheline, *Marguerite Duras*, Amsterdam, Rodopi, 1985.

25. Steinmetz-Schünemann, Helga, 'Marguerite Duras', in W.D. Lange, *Französische Literatur der Gegenwart*, Stuttgart, Alfred Kröner, 1971.

26. Vircondelet, Alain, *Marguerite Duras ou le temps de détruire*, Seghers, 1972.

27. Willis, Sharon, *Marguerite Duras: Writing on the Body*, University of Illinois Press, 1987.

Articles and Interviews

28. Guers-Villate, Yvonne, 'Les Personnages durassiens et le temps', *Neophilologus*, Vol. 66, no.3 (1982), pp.360–66.

29. Entretien avec Marguerite Duras, *Le Nouvel Observateur*, 28 September 1984, p.93.

30. *Libération*, 4 September 1984, pp.28–29.

31. Marini, Marcelle, 'Une femme sans aveu', *L'Arc*, no. 98 (1985), pp.6–16.

32. Narboni, Jean et Rivette, Jacques, 'La Destruction, la parole', *Cahiers du cinéma*, no.217 (November 1969), pp.45–60.

33. Noguez, Dominique, 'La Gloire des mots', *L'Arc*, no.98 (1985), pp.25–39.

General Studies

34. Flax, Jane, 'Mother/Daughter Relationships: Psychodynamics, Politics and Philosophy', in H. Eisenstein & A. Jardine, *The Future of Difference*, Boston, G.K. Hall, 1980.

35. Fowler, Roger, *Linguistics and the Novel*, London, Methuen, 1977.

36. Griffin-Crowder, Diane, 'The Semiotic Function of Ideology in Literary Discourse', *Bucknell Review*, Vol. 27, no.1 (1982), pp.157–68.

37. Hirsch, Marianne, 'Review Essay: Mothers and Daughters', *Signs*, Vol.7, no.1 (Autumn 1981), pp.200–23.

38. Josipovici, Gabriel, *The Lessons of Modernism*, London, Macmillan, 1977.
39. Lejeune, Phillipe, *Le Pacte autobiographique*, Eds du Seuil, 1975.
40. Lodge, David, *The Modes of Modern Writing*, London, Edward Arnold, 1977.
41. Penelope, Julia & Wolfe, Susan, 'Consciousness as Style: Style as Aesthetic', in B. Thorne, C. Kramerae, N. Henley (eds), *Language, Gender and Society*, Rowley, Mass., Newbury House Publishers, 1983, pp.125–40.
42. Rich, Adrienne, *Of Woman Born*, London, Virago, 1977.
43. Ullmann, Stephen, *Style in the French Novel*, Oxford, Basil Blackwell, 1964.

CRITICAL GUIDES TO FRENCH TEXTS

edited by
Roger Little, Wolfgang van Emden, David Williams

61. **Geoffrey N. Bromiley.** Thomas's Tristan *and the* Folie Tristan d'Oxford.
62. **R.J. Howells.** Rousseau: Julie ou la Nouvelle Héloïse.
63. **George Evans.** Lesage: Crispin rival de son maître *and* Turcaret.
64. **Paul Reed.** Sartre: La Nausée.
65. **Roger Mclure.** Sarraute: Le Planétarium.
66. **Denis Boak.** Sartre: Les Mots.
67. **Pamela M. Moores.** Vallès: L'Enfant.
68. **Simon Davies.** Laclos: Les Liaisons dangereuses.
69. **Keith Beaumont.** Jarry: Ubu Roi.
70. **G.J. Mallinson.** Molière: L'Avare.
71. **Susan Taylor-Horrex.** Verlaine: Fêtes galantes *and* Romances sans paroles.
72. **Malcolm Cook.** Lesage: Gil Blas.
73. **Sheila Bell.** Sarraute: Portrait d'un inconnu *and* Vous les entendez?
74. **W.D. Howarth.** Corneille: Le Cid.
75. **Peter Jimack.** Diderot: Supplément au Voyage de Bougainville.
76. **Christopher Lloyd.** Maupassant: Bel-Ami.
77. **David H. Walker.** Gide: Les Nourritures terrestres *and* La Symphonie pastorale
78. **Noël Peacock.** Molière: Les Femmes savantes.
79. **Jean H. Duffy.** Butor: La Modification.
80. **J.P. Little.** Genet: Les Nègres.
81. **John Campbell.** Racine: Britannicus.
82. **Malcolm Quainton.** D'Aubigné: Les Tragiques.
83. **Henry Phillips.** Racine: Mithridate.
84. **S. Beynon John.** Saint-Exupéry: Vol de Nuit *and* Terre des hommes.
85. **John Trethewey.** Corneille: L'Illusion comique *and* Le Menteur.
86. **John Dunkley.** Beaumarchais: Le Barbier de Séville.
87. **Valerie Minogue.** Zola: L'Assommoir.
88. **Kathleen Hall.** Rabelais: Pantagruel and Gargantua.